Sewing
911

Sewing
911

Practical and
Creative Rescues
for
Sewing Emergencies

Barbara Deckert

The Taunton Press

The Taunton Press
Inspiration for hands-on living™

The Taunton Press, Inc., 63 South Main Street, PO Box 5506, Newtown, CT 06470-5506
e-mail: tp@taunton.com

Distributed by Publishers Group West

DESIGN: Gloria Melfi

LAYOUT: Cathy Cassidy

ILLUSTRATOR: Ron Carboni

BACK COVER PHOTOGRAPHER: Jack Deutsch

INTERIOR PHOTOGRAPHERS: Jack Deutsch and Scott Phillips

LIBRARY OF CONGRESS CATALOGING-IN PUBLICATION DATA:
Deckert, Barbara
    Sewing 911 : practical and creative rescues for sewing emergencies / Barbara Deckert.
        p. cm.
    Includes index.
    ISBN 1-56158-444-4
    1. Clothing and dress--Repairing. 2. Clothing and dress--Alteration. 3. Sewing. I. Title.

TT720 .D43 2001
646'.6--dc21   2001027150

Printed in Malaysia
10 9 8 7 6 5 4 3 2 1

> *"Craftsmanship is the fine art of covering up your mistakes."*
> *—A plumber*

Contents

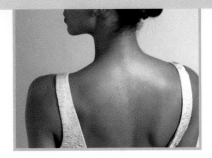

Introduction

Do you have sewing emergencies? We all do, no matter how well we sew or how many years we've been sewing. Mistakes just happen, and they always seem to happen when it's least convenient. The phone rings and while you're screening the call, you accidentally cut off a hem allowance on a skirt. Your toddler sneaks up behind you and tugs at your sleeve just as you're clipping open the ends of a welt pocket. It's 6 P.M. the day of your daughter's prom, she's hovering over you in electric curlers and hysterics, and you run out of the right color of thread to topstitch the hem of her dress. The circuit board in your electronic sewing machine shorts out in the middle of your last keyhole buttonhole on the new jacket that you wanted to wear for the big meeting in the morning. So what's a sewer to do?

As in any emergency, when we make a sewing mistake it's easy to succumb to panic and exasperation. For our common medical problems, like a sprained ankle or a bout with the flu, most of us are prepared with a little basic knowledge of first aid, some elastic bandages, and canned chicken soup. Sewers also need to keep remedies and supplies handy for their sewing disasters. This book is a first-aid manual for sewers.

Please note that you will find few if any "you should have dones" in this book. Hindsight is always clear! Nor will you find many admonitions to "rip and resew," since that's a straightforward solution to a sewing error that just won't help in many situations. What you will find here are practical and easy-to-follow instructions for other methods of "saving the patient," that is, the labor and materials you have invested in your sewing project.

Some of the treatments in this book are quick and simple. Some are more elaborate and creative. You get to choose how much effort you wish to put into your sewing emergency, and that will depend on the monetary and emotional value of the project. Remember that while not every "patient" can be saved, most can. Knowing how to fix your mistakes will help you sew with calm and confidence.

ACCIDENTAL FABRIC INJURIES

Treatments for accidental injuries in the form of fabric flaws, holes, cuts, and tears are all similar. In general, holes need to be covered with a patch, and cuts and tears need to be mended. There are several ways to accomplish both patches and mends.

what's inside

Flaws and Holes

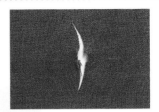

Rips and Snips

Overly Enthusiastic
Clipping and Trimming

"You would appreciate my sewing-disaster save I made last weekend," e-mailed my editor Sarah Coe. "I was making a blouse out of silk chiffon, and as usual, I cut a hole through it. It is sheer fabric with polka dots, so I made a little polka dot out of fusible interfacing and stuck it over the snip from the wrong side. I'm hoping people will just think their eyes are bothering them."

Flaws and Holes

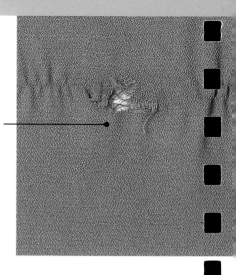

Holes happen. It is so easy not to notice a fabric flaw until a garment is cut; to find a moth hole in carefully stashed woolens; to catch the elbow of a favorite silk blouse on a protruding nail; or to accidentally cut an extra fold of fabric as you clip a seam. Instead of throwing the garment or sewing project away, try the following treatments.

Solution
Patches

Patches are typically made with matching fabric. If you don't have any scraps left, you can often scavenge a piece of matching fabric from the garment. Here are some places to look:

◆ Pocket bags and the area underneath the lower part of a patch pocket. Replace the purloined patch material with another fabric. Yes, you will need to patch the patch with some other fabric.

◆ Hem allowances. Replace the allowance with a narrower hem, with bias binding pressed open and applied like a facing, or another hem treatment (see pp. 23-24).

◆ Pleat underlaps. If pleats on a skirt, for example, are quite deep, you may be able to sneak an inch or two of fabric at the inside fold of the underlap toward the top of the pleat, where it is not likely to fly open with movement and show. Replace with another fabric.

◆ Facings. Make the facing narrower, replace it with purchased bias binding, roll-hem the neckline by hand or machine, or cover the neckline with trim.

Mending Older Clothes

You can use all of the patching and mending techniques discussed in this chapter on your older clothes to extend their wear. Have you seen old photos of men standing in dole lines or soup kitchen lines during the Great Depression? The clothes of these desperate, unemployed, hungry people are all remarkably clean, mended, and well pressed: They would make the crowd at your local upscale mall look like ragamuffins. From that time through World War II, when clothing and fabric were rationed, good citizens were encouraged to "use it up, wear it out, make it do, or do without." Patching and mending were points of pride, both personal and national.

Yet nowadays, we live in a world of disposable clothing. Much of the ready-to-wear clothing we buy has been mass-manufactured in underdeveloped countries by cheap and even by slave labor. So if you tear a hole in a $10 T-shirt, is it worth your time to mend or should you just throw it away? Well, that depends on the T-shirt and on your values. If the rest of the shirt is in good shape, mend it. If it's worn, mend it or not, but wear it while working around the house or yard. If it's worn and torn, use it as a cleaning or dusting cloth. Remember, a shirt is not just something you wear; it is a little bit of a laborer's life, and it is a little bit of Mother Nature's resources.

On a busy print, this patch is nearly invisible.

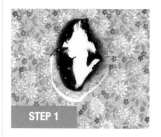

STEP 1

STEP 3

STEP 5

Self-fabric underpatches and fusible bonding web

1 Trim the hole as little as possible to remove burned or frayed edges.

2 Cut a patch of matching fabric about ½ in. larger all around than the hole. Match patterns if needed.

3 Place the hole wrong side up on your ironing board, then cut a piece of paper-backed bonding web the size of the patch. Center the fusible, paper side up, over the hole. Use the tip of your iron to fuse it all around the hole, being sure to avoid the hole itself so that the fusible does not stick to your ironing board.

4 Next, remove the paper backing. Trim any fusible web from inside the hole area. Don't worry if bits are left around the edges; they will be all but unnoticeable when the patch is complete.

5 Center the fabric patch, wrong side up, over the web, remembering to match any patterns. Cover with a press cloth and fuse according to instructions.

> **TIP** Spread the area you are repairing over a pressing ham to raise it up and away from the rest of the garment. It will be easier to see, access, and press.

Self-fabric overpatches and fusible bonding web

1 Start by cutting a matching piece of fabric larger than the hole. Match patterns as needed.

2 Fuse the patch's wrong side to the paper-backed bonding material.

3 Next, trim the patch to cover the hole, plus about a ½-in. margin all around. Remove the paper backing.

4 Center the patch over the hole, web side down, cover with a press cloth, and press.

Carefully matched patterns on this overpatch make it unobstrusive.

Darning with a patch

Darning is what our frugal grandmothers did for holes in socks and overalls to keep them serviceable. You can darn wounds in your sewing projects either by hand or machine. First, apply an underpatch or overpatch as explained on the facing page. If you don't have a fusing agent handy, just pin or hand-baste the patch in place.

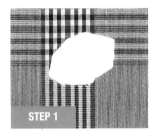

STEP 1

♦ By machine, use a short straight stitch or zigzag and matching thread to sew rows of closely spaced stitching up and down and back and forth over the patch area. Just use the reverse control on your machine; don't bother with precise spacing, pivoting, and so on. Cover the patch with random rows of stitches in all directions. Alternatively, lower the feed dogs on your machine, center the hole in an embroidery hoop to stabilize the fabric, and sew the rows of stitches with a darning foot while guiding the fabric under the needle by hand. The stitching made with either method of machine-darning helps secure the patch to make it extra sturdy, which is a plus for durable, wash-and-wear garments. The stitches can even help the patch blend in with the rest of the garment, particularly for prints (see the top photos on p.10).

STEP 2

Machine-darning makes patches extra durable.

Without a patch, use a stabilizer to back the hole.

◆ By hand, use closely spaced rows of small running stitches as explained on p. 9 to darn.

TIP Try using combinations of thread colors **for** darning to blend in with the fabric's colors.

Darning without a patch

If you do not have scraps of matching fabric available, you can still darn a hole. This is the traditional method of darning, and it is especially suitable for knits and fine garments.

◆ By machine, darn as described for darning with a patch, but baste a tearaway or water-soluble stabilizer under the hole (see the photo at left). The rows of stitches need to be close enough together and numerous enough to form a "fabric" that will cover the hole. After darning, remove the stabilizer (see the bottom photo at left).

◆ By hand, spread the hole over something to support it. Our ancestors used darning eggs, which looked like wooden baby rattles that didn't rattle. A hard-boiled egg, a small, smooth stone, or the side or bottom of a tumbler is a good substitute. Stitch a small running stitch around the hole's edges, then stitch through about ½ in. at the hole's edge, bring the thread to the opposite side of the hole, and stitch another ½ in. Repeat with close rows of stitches (see the top photo on the facing page). Secure and cut the thread end, then turn your work 90 degrees. About ½ in. from the perimeter of the hole, secure the end of the thread by taking a few tiny stitches right on top of each other. Next, sew a small running stitch from the perimeter to the hole itself at

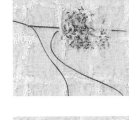

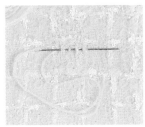

right angles to your first rows of stitches. As you reach the hole, "weave" the needle under and over the threads that cover the hole (see the center photo at right). The finely spaced rows of stitches will form a fabric to cover the hole.

> **TIP** For an almost invisible repair on heavy knits or tweeds, pull threads from a cut edge and thread them through a needle to darn the hole by hand.

Contrast thread is shown above for clarity.

Solution
Appliqués

If life gives you lemons, of course you make lemonade. When life gives sewers holes in garments that are too big or conspicuous to patch, we make appliqués. An appliqué is simply a patch that is meant to be decorative. You can apply appliqués by machine, by hand, or by using fusibles.

Bonding agent and fabric motif

① For printed fabrics, select an individual motif that is large enough to cover the hole completely or that will match the damaged area and cover the hole. If you don't have matching fabric, try a contrast color, pick up one of the other colors in the fabric's print or trim, or try finding a coordinating print motif. Cut out the motif with a generous ½-in. margin all around.

STEP 1

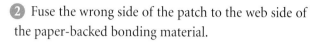

STEP 4

2 Fuse the wrong side of the patch to the web side of the paper-backed bonding material.

3 Trim the patch to the shape of the motif, then peel off the backing.

4 Using a press cloth, fuse the motif, right sides up, over the hole.

"A customer once brought me a flimsy piece of printed rayon that had quite a few flaws. I carefully cut around them, or so I thought, until I discovered at the first fitting that there was a very noticeable hole on the front of the tunic. I covered the hole with a little flower that was part of the print, and neither of us could tell."

STEP 1

Reverse appliqué

1 Using contrasting fabric, pin or hand-baste an under-patch that is larger than the hole.

2 Satin-stitch through both layers by machine in a decorative shape around the hole. The shape could be a basic geometric design like a heart, triangle, or circle, or a shape that echoes the patterns in a print.

STEP 2

3 Use sharp-pointed scissors to carefully trim away the top layer of garment fabric only close to the stitches.

Peekaboos

Peekaboos are simply holes that you finish to make them look as if you planned them.

STEP 3

Variations

More Appliqué Ideas

- ◆ *Use a purchased appliqué.*

- ◆ *Secure the appliqué using a machine satin stitch or blanket stitch, or slipstitch by hand.*

- ◆ *Place matching or similar appliqués on other parts of the garment to add to the design.*

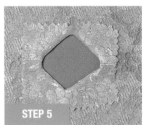

STEP 3

STEP 5

❶ Trim the hole so that it is the size and shape that you want, such as a simple geometric shape.

❷ Make a facing for the hole by cutting a piece of matching or similar fabric about 2 in. larger than the hole and about the same shape, then finish the outside edges.

❸ Next, center the facing over the hole, right sides together, and stitch around the hole with small stitches and a ¼-in. seam.

❹ Clip, turn, understitch, and press the peekaboo's facing.

❺ Fuse or catchstitch the facing in place on the wrong side of the garment.

Alternatively, you could finish the raw edge of the hole by using a machine zigzag, overcasting by hand, applying seam sealant sparingly, and then applying decorative trim to cover the edges of the peekaboo appliqué (see the center photo at right).

TIP

Holes in lace, even the most fragile, can be patched almost invisibly. Use a motif cut from the same lace or from another lace that will blend with the colors and textures of the garment. Match patterns if possible. Slipstitch the motif over the hole by hand, preferably with silk thread.

Rips and Snips

For clean cuts or tears, because there is no expanse of hole to cover, a narrow seam will normally repair the damage done by errant snips and rips.

66 *I once completed a beautiful, Victorian-style, custom wedding gown that was made out of a very wiggly and slippery silk charmeuse. Sewing on that fabric was like sewing on spider webs that have been sprayed with WD-40. Sure enough, as I clipped an errant thread, I managed to snip a ½-in. slit in the front of the gathered skirt, about 1 in. from the waist seam. After cussing in four languages and bursting into tears, I mended the cut and then concealed it in the gathers at the waist seam. Nobody knew but us chickens.* 99

Solution
Mending

Mending is another of the almost but not quite lost domestic arts. Women used to keep mountainous piles of holey clothes that needed repairs in their work baskets and would mend by hand while listening to the radio or watching TV in the evenings. When we go to the trouble to make a garment ourselves, surely errant rips and snips are worth the little time it takes to mend. With modern materials and machines, mending is easier and faster than it used to be.

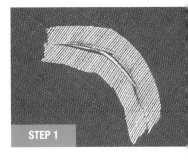

STEP 1

1. Reinforce the edges of the cut or tear with narrow pieces of fusible interfacing. Match the weight of the interfacing to your fabric.

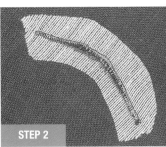

2. Fold the cut right sides together, then using a small straightstitch, sew the cut edges together in as narrow a seam as possible. Taper the seam to the folds of fabric at each end of the mend, as you would sew a dart.

3. Use a narrow, short zigzag to finish the raw edges of the cut together and to add durability.

STEP 2

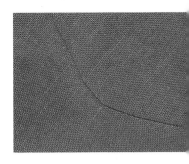

4. Press the seam to one side, avoiding the ends, as you would press a dart.

“*A woman with 30 years of sewing experience shared the following: She was charged with repairing the wedding dress of her best friend's daughter. The gown was lace underlined with satin, but the lace only had a big stain on the front midriff area. She planned to remove the stained lace and replace it with something similar. Instead of just trimming off the stained lace, however, she managed to cut through both layers of fabric from side seam to side seam. 'I was hysterical. I called my friend and told her that I had cut the wedding dress in half!' After everyone calmed down, she repaired the cut using a narrow seam as described above, and disguised it as an Empire bodice seam, with matching trim over the mend and at the waist seam of the dress so it would look like part of the design. 'It turned out looking really good and not at all like the product of disaster control. Unfortunately, the dress worked better than the marriage did—but that's another story.'*”

Variations

More Mending Ideas

◆ *Disguise the mend. You may even want to lengthen it so it looks like a planned seam. If needed for symmetry or to make the mend look like a planned dart, seam, or other design feature, you can make a similar seam on the opposite side of the garment.*

◆ *Hide the mend. If the mend is close to gathers or pleats, try rearranging the fabric so that the mend falls to the inside of a gather, pleat, dart, or tuck. For symmetry, you may need to make similar adjustments on the other side of the garment piece.*

◆ *Use appliqué or trim to cover the mend. This is especially useful when you have cut up a foldline or chopped off a hem allowance.*

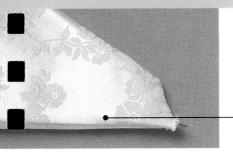

Overly Enthusiastic Clipping and Trimming

Of course, sewers want tidy, flat, and thin inside seams and curved seams that take the shape we desire when we turn them right side out, so we trim and clip, sometimes too much. Do not despair if you turn a collar inside out and energetically poke the tips of your scissors through a corner. This type of thing is easy to fix.

Solution
Suturing accidental lacerations

1. Reinforce the area of the broken stitching with small pieces of a lightweight fusible interfacing.

2. Next, overstitch with small stitches, just deep enough inside the original seamline to clear the accidental clip or poke-through.

3. If needed for symmetry, make a similar adjustment on the opposite side of the garment piece. For example, if you resew one collar point, remember to resew the other one in the same manner so they will look alike on the finished garment.

2
SHORTAGES

You know how this one goes. When you find a fabric at the sewing store that is perfect for a particular pattern, there is always less left on the bolt than whatever you need. No, the store can't order any more. Or you pull that beautiful piece of goods from your stash and plan a brilliant garment for it, but you lay out the pattern pieces and run unfailingly short. I have absentmindedly sewn one too many respaced buttonholes on a blouse, only to find that I was consequently missing an extra button for that extra hole. Luckily, there are a number of ways to make do with whatever materials you have on hand.

Instead of dashing back to the store in hopes that there may be more of your fabric and trim left and then as often as not finding out otherwise, it's often easier and faster to try some of the following tricks.

what's inside

Not Enough Fabric

Not Enough Buttons

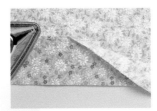
Not Enough Thread

"As a young girl, a dressmaker friend of mine embarked on sewing a dress from a beautiful piece of black and white printed cotton. When she started cutting out the pattern, she discovered that one large pattern piece would not fit with the design going in the right direction. As my friend was loudly berating herself for her stupidity, an elderly neighbor arrived for a visit. The neighbor dismissed her self-pity with the wise advice– 'Just put the piece in the back, and walk away fast, dear.'"

Not Enough Fabric

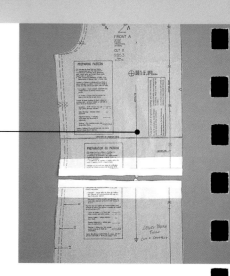

Which of the following techniques for dealing with fabric shortages you will choose will depend on how short you are on fabric, the size of the pattern pieces for your garment, and the surface design of your fabric. Instead of analyzing these complicated factors, just think through several options until you find the one that will work best for you. Directional prints and border prints will force you to make hard decisions when you encounter fabric shortages, but most can be handled by using the following basic techniques.

Before you start to panic about fabric famines, try laying out your garment differently from what the pattern instructs. Remember that the pattern's layout works for a range of sizes, and your size could be at the smaller or larger end of that range, so there is often more fabric to work with than you might think. Ignore the layout diagram. Start by laying out the big pattern pieces first, paying attention to grain, nap, and so on as you normally would. Then try it again another way. When you get the big pieces placed most efficiently, then fit the small pieces in. Don't be afraid to squeeze the pieces together very closely.

Solution
Place some garment pieces on the crossgrain

Generally, pieces cut on the crossgrain seem slightly firmer and more springy than when cut on the lengthwise grain, so they do not drape as softly. That's because as the fabric is woven, the lengthwise threads, or warp, are under tremendous tension, while the crosswise threads, or weft, are held under less tension. That's also why fabric cut on the lengthwise grain typically stretches little if at all after it is woven, but fabric cut on the crossgrain has some give.

> **TIP** If you're working with a piece of fabric that no longer has its selvages and you want to determine its grain directions, pull a thread from each direction of the weave. Typically, if you break the thread and it "snaps" or "pops," that thread is from the lengthwise grain. If you break the thread and it shreds, it is probably from the crossgrain. The variations in tension during the weaving process cause this difference.

So if you cut a skirt on the crossgrain, for instance, those relatively wiry lengthwise threads are now running horizontally, and they act like springs that support the softer crossgrain threads. Therefore, the piece does not drape as well as when cut on the lengthwise grain. To test this effect, hold the fabric by the selvage and then by the cut edges to judge the drape. Which is most suitable for your garment? A full, gathered, organza skirt for a ball gown, for example, might drape beautifully cut on the crossgrain, while a pair of classic, pleated worsted wool gabardine trousers might really need to be cut on the lengthwise grain to drape gracefully. If the printed or woven pattern of your fabric is directional, like a stripe, try placing yokes, collars, flaps, contrast bands, cuffs, and so on on the crossgrain. Look at the difference in directions, and decide if you like the resulting design.

Solution
Cut some garment pieces slightly off grain

The ready-to-wear industry routinely cuts some garment pieces slightly off grain. The best pieces to try this with are small pieces that will be interfaced with a fusible interfacing, such as collars, facings, cuffs, yokes, contrast bands, and patch pockets. The stiffness of the interfacing helps counteract the effect of gravity on the fabric.

Other garment pieces that do not merely hang freely from one point on the body, such as the way a chemise front and back hang freely from the shoulders, are also suitable because their off-grain drape will be relatively less noticeable. Some examples are sleeves with gathers or cuffs at the wrist, bodices with waist seams or those to be worn tucked into pants or a skirt, bodices gathered into shoulder yokes, pegged hems and bubble skirts, and harem pants, sweat pants, and cuffed knickers and bloomers. Don't laugh; for the next winter's fashion season, we may all be wearing gray flannel bloomers to the office with our stiletto heels.

Solution
Eliminate the hem allowance

Eliminate a hem allowance by cutting it off the pattern piece or folding the tissue at the hemline and pinning it out of the way. Here are some ideas for substitutes for a standard hem allowance:

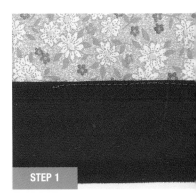

STEP 1

A faced hem

Use a 2-in.-wide bias strip of a coordinating fabric, or use purchased bias binding that has been gently pressed flat.

1 Sew the facing or binding, right sides together, to the hemline in a ¼-in. seam.

2 Gently press the seam toward the binding, taking care not to stretch the bias facing.

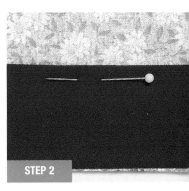

STEP 2

3 If desired, understitch the facing.

4 Turn the facing to the inside, press lightly, and hem as usual.

A trimmed hem

For a trimmed hem, select a trim that is at least ½ in. wide. Try using lace hem tape, other flat lace trim, or any other lightweight, flexible trim, such as braid or even jumbo rickrack. You can apply the trim to the right side of the hem if you like the look or to the wrong side for a little secret pleasure.

STEP 4

1 Lap the trim by ¼ in. over the right side of the hem edge for trims that will show on the wrong side of the garment, or lap the trim over the wrong side of the hem edge for trim that will show on the right side of the garment.

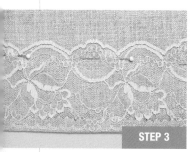

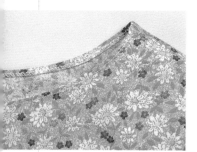

STEP 3

A narrow topstitched hem.

A lettuce-leaf hem.

An overlock rolled hem.

A hand-rolled hem.

2 Stitch in place.

3 Turn the trim to the desired side, press, and topstitch in place or hemstitch by hand.

> **TIP** Try a trimmed hem for evening skirts and gowns that are full, such as circle skirts, gored skirts, and gathered skirts. Instead of decorative trim, use nylon braid, sometimes called "horsehair braid" because that's what it was originally made of. This braid is available in several widths and is woven on the bias so it is flexible but also firm and springy. It supports and increases the flare of a full skirt.

Narrow topstitched or rolled hem

Use your serger to sew a narrow, rolled hem with matching or contrasting thread. For knits, use a fine overlock or rolled hem stitch, and stretch the fabric under the foot as you sew for a lettuce-leaf hem. On a conventional machine, sew a narrow topstitched hem. For luxury garments made of soft fabrics, roll the hem by hand.

Solution
Eliminate some garment length

I am not going to suggest that you turn your floor-dusting bell bottoms into hot pants or your hip-length tunic into a belly-button-baring crop top. There are plenty of easy ways to conserve fabric *and* retain the look you desire.

Adjust your pattern for lengths

Always remember to adjust your pattern for length before you lay it out. For example, if you are 5'1" and your Misses pattern is drafted for someone who is 5'6" tall, you know you have 5 in. of extra length times whatever multiple of main pattern pieces you are working with. The extra length that you have to work with lies somewhere on the pattern pieces between your toes and neck and between the top and the bottom of the garment in question. Compare all of your body lengths, such as back waist, crotch, sleeve, desired outseam, and side seam, to those of the pattern pieces to determine exactly where on the pattern you can eliminate extra length.

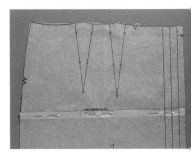

Adjust the pattern to your body lengths before you cut.

TIP Do not assume that you know **where on your pattern pieces you can safely eliminate extra length**. Our bodies are unique. Some of us have short torsos and long legs or long rises and short legs, and so on. Measure and make sure!

Eliminate some length by design

Would you still like the garment if it had short sleeves instead of long? Could you live with a below-the-knee hem instead of an above-ankle hem? Do you really need cuffs on those tailored pants? If you can be flexible about design, you can still sew a satisfying and useful garment even when you don't have enough fabric for your original idea.

Hidden areas of garments can be cut from contrast fabrics.

"I once made a raw-silk tweed, four-piece suit for a rather formidable lady lawyer. Of course, she did not bring me enough fabric. Although I can usually squeeze blood out of a turnip, there was no way that I could lay out all four garments, even though I tried for hours to do so. I figured that among the individual garments—jacket, short and straight skirt, vest, and pants—that the pants were the least likely to be part of her more formal work wardrobe, so I asked her if she would be interested in walking shorts or mid-calf gaucho pants. She went for the gaucho pants, and she later told me that she always received compliments on them and was considered quite the fashion plate in her office."

Eliminate length where it won't show

If a blouse will always be worn tucked in, for example, cut off the bottom of the blouse, front and back, about 2 in. below the waistline. Add seam allowances to the upper and lower bodice sections, but cut the lower bodice sections from a different fabric, since it won't show while worn. This would also work for a skirt with a hip yoke that would always be worn with an over-blouse or jacket that would cover the yoke.

> **TIP** If you desire more length on the garment than your fabric allows, see "Too Short" on pp. 76-80.

Solution
Eliminate some design width

Many garments use extra fabric to add fullness as a part of the design, often in the form of gathers, pleats, and released tucks. You can sometimes eliminate some width on a pattern piece to make gathers less full or pleats shallower. Simply fold out a lengthwise pleat in the pattern piece to eliminate extra width where desired.

Bear in mind that if you eliminate some width, you will also likely change the appearance of the garment and that change may or may not be what you want. For an extreme example, if you have a pattern for a very fully gathered chiffon evening skirt that you want to use for a stiff fabric, such as duchesse satin, you could easily eliminate up to one-third of the width on the front and back skirt pattern pieces. There will still be plenty of fullness for pleasing gathers. On the other hand, if you used a medium-weight fabric, such as a wool challis, eliminating as much as one-third of the front and back width might make the gathers look skimpy.

Often pleats in ready-to-wear are quite shallow, and the reason is simply to save fabric and increase profits. You can make pleats shallower, too, by folding out some width on the tissue along the length of several or each of the pleats' underlaps.

Folding out a decorative pleat on this shirt front saved some fabric.

> **TIP** The situations that do not have pat answers become a question of judgment, taste, and desperation.

On the other hand, note that you must not eliminate design or wearing ease altogether. Garments that are short on width will be uncomfortable, will not wear well, and may emphasize the fullness of our convex curves (bellies, busts, upper arms, and fannies), since fabric would stretch tautly across these areas if there is too little ease, instead of gracefully draping over them. Just think about the consequences of eliminating some width when you are short of fabric; it might not matter much at all.

Solution
Eliminate some garment pieces

Would you still like the garment if it did not have a collar, cuffs, sleeves, flaps, patch pockets, overdrapes, and so on? Sometimes a fabric can be so ornamental by itself that eliminating some design details allows its beauty to be the star of your design. Also, particularly in years when "minimalism" is popular, sometimes eliminating details can make a garment look edgy and sharp.

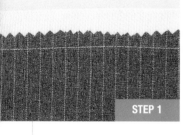

STEP 1

STEP 3

To substitute for a waistband

Instead of a waistband, try using a grosgrain ribbon band.

1. Lap ⅞-in. grosgrain ribbon just over the waist seamline, and topstitch it in place close to the ribbon's edge.

2. Turn the ribbon to the wrong side and press.

3. Tack the lower edge of the ribbon to the inside of the garment at the seams, zipper tape, and darts. Alternately, you can topstitch the ribbon facing in place from the right side of the skirt or pants.

To substitute for cuffs, collars, and other design treatments

To finish a neckline without a collar or facing, you can sew a narrow rolled hem by hand or machine, you could apply bias binding that is folded to the wrong side, or you could apply a French binding. Instead of cuffs, some other ways of finishing the raw edge of a sleeve are by using a hand or machine rolled hem, a narrow top-stitched hem, or a bias or French binding.

To hold the fullness of a sleeve around the wrist, you can apply a bias binding that is turned to the wrong side and topstitched in place to form a casing for elastic or a bias tubing drawstring (see the top photo on p. 30).

A French binding is a tidy finish for raw edges.

Sewing a French Binding

A French binding is simply a bias binding that is double folded. It is suitable for medium-weight to lightweight fabrics and is actually faster to sew than a standard bias binding because there is less pressing required.

To make one, start by cutting a strip of bias a generous four times the desired finished width, plus two ¼-in. seam allowances, and the length that you need. Fold the binding in half lengthwise, and steam it gently without stretching, but do not press it flat. Baste the raw edges together just inside the ¼-in. seamline. With raw edges even, sew the binding to the right side of the garment in a ¼-in. seam, and clip any curves to release them. Next, fold the binding to the garment wrong side, and slipstitch the fold of the binding to the machine stitching.

Use your fingers to ease the binding in place to avoid drag lines. Gently steam the finished binding, and allow it to cool and dry before handling.

You could also simply fold out a couple of pleats at the outside of the wrist and hold them in place with buttons sewn through all layers (see the center photo at left).

To substitute for facings on double-breasted garments

Facings on double-breasted garments use a great deal of fabric. Try cutting the facing piece in half lengthwise, then add seam allowances and substitute another fabric for the half that is farthest from the finished opening of the garment. When worn, the substitution will not be visible.

Sleeves can be finished with elastic in casing or with a pleat and button.

Solution
Use a different fabric

Find a contrasting or coordinating fabric for some garment pieces, such as collars, cuffs, belts, pockets, flaps, yokes, and facings.

Be creative with your use of contrasting or coordinating fabrics. They will draw viewers' eyes to those interesting design details that make your garment a true original. You can try using some fabric from another garment that you are planning to wear with the one you are sewing. For example, for a top to wear with a particular pair of pants, use the coordinating pants' fabric on the top's patch pockets, yoke, cuffs, or collar for a sophisticated sportswear look.

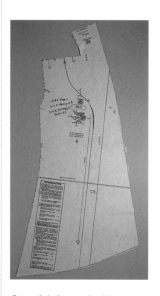

Save fabric on double-breasted facings by splitting the facing vertically, adding seam allowances, and cutting the inner piece from contrast.

Solution
Piece unobtrusively with matching fabric

Small scraps can be pieced to squeeze out that last garment piece.

It's often possible to piece garment components, that is, sew together two or three smaller pieces of fabric to form one main garment piece. This works well for darker fabrics or those with overall woven or printed patterns, since the joins may hardly be visible. Start by sewing together the scraps in straight seams with a narrow seam allowance, then finish the allowance to prevent raveling and press the seams open. Remember to carefully match patterns and grainlines. Next, pin the pattern piece on the larger, "new" piece of fabric, minding the grainlines, and cut it out.

Solution
Color-block with contrasting fabric

Color blocking is a design technique that can help save your day if you are short of fabric. Just use a contrasting or coordinating fabric for a selection of the pattern pieces. Here are some ideas:

◆ For a princess-lined jacket, try a dark fabric for the front and back side pieces and a brighter or lighter fabric for the front and back for a slenderizing effect. It worked for Princess Diana.

◆ For a 1960s geometric look, add center-front seams to a basic, jewel-necked, short-sleeved, hip-length top and basic A-line skirt. Alternate colors from right to left and from top to bottom. Try this in black and white for a graphically groovy checkerboard effect. Smile when your admirers holler, "Hey, baby!"

Not Enough Buttons

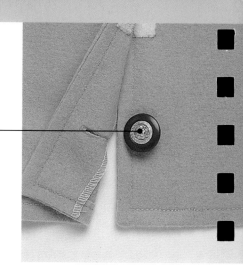

Either we count wrong, there are only two cards left of the perfect button for our project when of course we need three, or we respace the buttonholes and end up short of buttons. A little button juggling will fix this problem.

Solution
Space buttons more widely apart

To make the most of your buttons, space them more widely apart than whatever is called for by the pattern. To avoid "gaposis," use hook-and-loop tape "dots" or snaps on the wrong side of the overlap and on the right side of the underlap to secure the closure between buttons (see the photo above). Or sew buttonholes on the underlap between the more widely spaced fashion button locations, then sew a small, plain or clear button onto the wrong side of the overlap. Be careful that your stitches do not show through to the right side of the garment. When these buttons are buttoned, they will make the closure more secure but will not show on the closed, finished garment.

Solution
Use nonmatching buttons where they won't show

There are often buttons that are never seen on the finished garment, and they provide a perfect opportunity for substitution. Here are some ideas of where to use nonmatching buttons: at the waist if a belt will always be worn, below the waist if a shirt will always be tucked into pants or a skirt, and on the underlap of a double-breasted jacket.

Solution
Leave a button out if you won't really use it

Do you routinely button the top button at the neck of a menswear-style shirt? Are you going to actually button the lower buttons of a tunic below the full-hip level? Would you leave the last seven of the closely spaced 24 buttons on that shirt dress open below the knee anyway?

Solution
Mix and match buttons

Check your button box; just go for a combination that makes you smile. Try grouping buttons by colors that coordinate with your fabric, such as white, lavendar, and green buttons for a blouse with a lilacs-in-bloom print. Most metal buttons go well together, whether they are gold or silver finish. You could also group disparate buttons by themes: all old-fashioned and delicate, all bold and modern, all square shapes, or all with flower motifs.

Mix buttons of similar sizes and colors.

Not Enough Thread

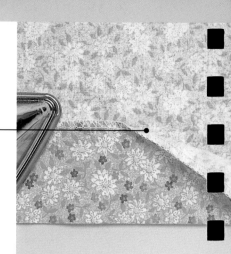

When you run out of matching thread and don't have the time or inclination to dash out and buy more, what can you do? Make the most of the thread you have by using the following techniques.

Solution
Use the right color in the needle only

If you think you are running low on thread, instead of rewinding the bobbin as needed with the matching thread, use whatever color thread that you have on hand that's closest in color. Mid-grays and beiges blend well with many colors. If you run out of needle thread abruptly, simply remove the bobbin, place it on the spool pin, thread the machine as usual, and substitute another bobbin thread.

TIP

When you realize that you might run short on thread, save your matching thread for stitching that will show, such as topstitching.

Solution
Blend threads to match

Sometimes you can combine two or three colors of thread on extra spool pins to blend in with the fabric's tones and textures. For example, for a gray tweed, try blending black and off-white threads.

Two thread colors blend best on this heathery worsted,

Solution
Pull threads from the fabric's cut ends

For nearly invisible hand-darning and hemming, thread individual yarns into a needle for a perfect match on expensive garments. This is not a technique that you are going to want to use to hand-hem a circle skirt with a circumference of 5 yd., but to hem a tweedy little sleeve or a little straight skirt in a hard-to-match color, it works beautifully. Threads pulled from the crossgrain tend to break easily, so sew gently, slowly, and wax your thread.

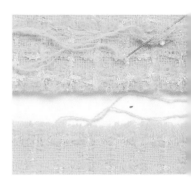

Threads pulled from fabric match perfectly.

Solution
Substitute fusibles for thread

When you're out of time as well as thread, use fusible products to secure hems and facings. When you do have the time and the thread, stitch them for extra security. I really have nothing personal against fusibles. It's just that they are often stiffer than machine or hand stitches, and they do tend to come loose as a garment ages. I hate mending, so I would rather take two minutes to stitch something securely in the first place than take 12 minutes a year later to repair a fused hem that has pulled loose.

If all else fails, fuse.

3

DEFECTIVE DESIGN DETAILS

I f God is in the details, then sewers stumble toward the salvation of success through the obstacles of design details. It is so easy to take a beautiful piece of fabric, cut it out wisely, fit it well, and then ruin the garment's effect with a pucker here, a curl there, or a droop where there ought to be drape. We could simply avoid all those sometimes tricky collars, lapels, flaps, layered hemlines, welts, bindings, and so on, but our clothing would be very, very boring.

In fact, many sewers avoid all but the plainest of patterns. Yes, we are all short of time, but sometimes we just aren't quite confident about our ability to sew all the little particulars that make clothes interesting and satisfying to wear. But "if it isn't any work," as my grandmother used to say, "it probably isn't worth doing." So fear not; choose a more complicated pattern than whatever you have sewn before, and enjoy the challenge! Fortunately, most of the little boo-boos that we make with the details of our sewing projects can heal, so we can feel much better when they do.

what's inside

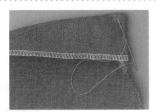

Lopsided Laps and **Lower Edges**

Uneven Hemlines on Layered Skirts and Dresses

Wounded Welts

Fixing Flap Fatigue

Flipping, Flopping, Puckering, and Pulling

Bungled Buttonholes

Mismatched Plaids and Patterns

> *One of my 'expensive mistakes' photos from a major fashion magazine shows an embellished denim jacket priced at $1,118. There is a zipper running up the center front, and the lower edges of the fronts are uneven by a good ½ in. I would dearly love to include the names of the designers and fashion magazines for these mistakes, but it would not be wise.*

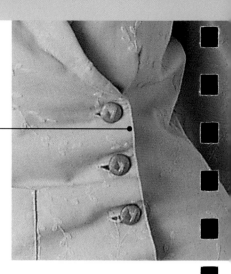

Lopsided Laps and Lower Edges

Have you ever sewn a jacket or blouse, completed the garment to the point where you are ready to add the buttons and buttonholes, and then realized that the two center fronts are not the same length? Here are some quick treatments for uneven lower edges.

Solution
Cheat it

Look at the garment's hemline and determine where the discrepancy will show the least. Just lap the right over the left openings (for women's wear) and tweak the closures as follows.

For a jacket with an even hemline that has lapels or a V-neck

The unevenness in the lengths of the laps will show least at the top of the opening. Keep the lower edges even, and ignore the extra length through the neck area. It will not be noticeable.

For a jacket with a center-front zip

If you have a jacket with a center-front zip that you will probably wear slightly open at the neck rather than zipped all the way up, cheat also at the top edge. Again, keep the bottom edges even, and allow one neck edge to be slightly shorter than the other.

On a garment with a shaped hem that opens up at the lower edge

On this type of garment, such as on a menswear-style vest, you can typically cheat at the bottom. The shaped edges will distract from the irregularity.

On a very long row of buttons

If you have a long row of buttons such as on a shirtwaist dress, you can carefully and evenly divide the excess length among all the spaces between the buttons or holes. This works well whether the overlap or the underlap is too long.

If the overlap is longer than the underlap

If you are lucky enough to get the overlap longer than the underlap, you can simply divide the excess length evenly at the top and bottom of the garment.

Overstitch the longer lap to correct.

Solution
Fix it

Sometimes the length of the finished opening edges on a garment can be so far off that, yes, you will need to resew.

Conventionally

Turn the facing wrong side out, then resew the longer of the laps to the desired length at either the top or the bottom of the garment. Stitch over the original stitching, sew the correction, and overstitch into the original seamline. Trim, turn, and press.

If you have already topstitched the openings

Break the topstitching in the center of the area to be corrected. Carefully pull out the stitches for a couple of inches in both directions without breaking the thread further. Pull the ends to the wrong side and knot to secure. Thread the ends through a needle, and slip it into the hole of the last stitch, between the fabric layers, out through the upper layer of fabric, and trim the excess thread to bury the tails. Next, turn the facing wrong side out and resew the corner as described above. Then topstitch the area to be corrected, starting precisely where the old topstitching ends. Pull those threads to the wrong side and knot to secure, then bury the tails. The topstitching will once again look continuous.

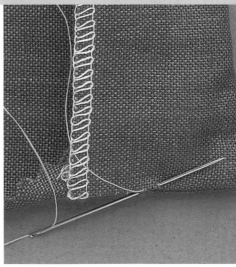

By hand

If your fabric is bulky or fuzzy, to shorten a lap you can simply use a hand needle to push in a little tuck at the longer lap's lower or upper horizontal seamline, which you can then slip-stitch in place. How much of a tuck you can get away with depends on the texture, bulk, and opacity of your fabric. On soft woolens, for example, an extra ¼ in. to ½ in. that ends up as seam allowance inside the garment will not be noticeable, but on a crisp, sheer linen, it might look like a conspicuous lump.

Tuck the seam inward with your needle and slipstitch in place.

Solution
Exaggerate it

If you are really, really off, then make the discrepancy look as if you planned it. Here are some ideas that will work for both shorter overlaps and underlaps.

For buttoned closures

Pull the overlap neckline down and the hemline up, and divide the extra space evenly among the buttons. The effect will be that of an asymmetric, edgy-looking top with poufs of fabric between the buttons that will form attractive, diagonal drape lines across the torso (see the photos on p. 38.)

If the opening is zippered

Try gathering or pleating the excess length at the opening edge, then sew the zipper to match the shorter side.

Solution
For double-breasted closures

On jackets, dresses, and coats, even when you sew the opening edges the same length, it's common to find that the lower inside edges of the underlay hang down longer than does the hem at the center front of the garment. This affliction has many causes, but there are a couple of very easy solutions.

Make sure that there is sufficient ease at the hips

If the garment does not drape over the hips easily, it will pull open at the center front, which will make the laps on a double-breasted garment look uneven. Let out the garment at the hips, and check for improvement.

Use adequate fasteners

Be sure to use fasteners in the right places on the inside of the garment between the laps. You must secure the weight of the underlap to the overlap with buttons, snaps, hook-and-loop tape, or even ribbon ties so it will not droop at the hemline. If needed, raise the position of the lowermost button on the inside of the garment's overlap to prevent the underlap from showing at the hemline when the garment is worn.

"I have dozens of photos of double-breasted garments costing thousands of dollars that suffer from improperly placed fasteners. The ones that are worn too tight at the hips show horizontal stress lines, and the ones with inadequate fasteners on the inside show the inside corner of the underlap drooping lower than the overlap."

Uneven Hemlines on Layered Skirts and Dresses

Have you ever sewn a lovely, very full, multiple-layered skirt in chiffon or georgette and been driven crazy by all the uneven hemlines? If the skirt is flared, the lower part of the seams are cut on the bias, so of course they stretch differently than the centers of the pieces that are on the straight grain. This results in a handkerchief-hem effect, whether you like it or not. Similar droopiness affects bias-cut skirts as well. Ripping and resewing hems as many times as it may take to get them right is likely to mar fragile fabrics and to drive you mad. If you end up with wobbly hems, try the following regimens.

Solution
If there is a waist seam

If there is a waist seam or other horizontal seam that holds the layers together, such as at a hip yoke, you can shorten an area of a longer layer with a minimum of ripping. Directly above the too-long area, remove the

43

stitching in the waist seam. Carefully pull the too-long layer upward until the lower edges are even, pin in place, and resew that part of the seam.

Adjust the long layer along a raw edge.

Solution
If there is no waist seam or if the fabric is too fragile to rip and resew

STEP 2

1 Allow the garment to hang on a dress form or shaped hanger for several days—the more the better. This will allow the bias to stretch out.

2 Carefully hand-baste all the layers together. Put the garment on the wearer, if possible, or leave it on the form or hanger. Baste all around the skirt or dress 1 in. or so from the hemline, while keeping the basting parallel to the floor.

3 Trim all of the layers even, as closely as possible to the original hemline.

4 Restitch all of the hems.

TIP

After you have all the layers hemmed evenly, store the garment flat. If you store it on the hanger, the bias will continue to stretch, and the next time you wear the garment the hems will likely be uneven.

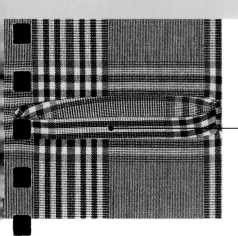

Wounded Welts

Let's face it: Welts and their flap mates look sharp, clean, and tailored, but they are a sewing challenge. The ready-to-wear industry uses besom pocket machines to make them perfectly. These dedicated machines cost so much (about $30,000) that not even all garment factories have them. We home sewers at all skill levels often botch welts: We come out with uneven welt widths, holes in the ends, fraying at the welt seams, or puckers in the corners. Sometimes the flaps for the welts come out the right size, but more often they are too long or too short. Sometimes with our enthusiasm for close trimming, it's impossible to safely rip and resew these details. But don't let wicked welts worry you. Here are some rescues for this type of sewing emergency.

TIP

Always apply fusible interfacing to the welt area before you sew the welt seams, and sew with very small stitches. The interfacing and the small stitch length will help prevent raveling and holes at the ends of the welts.

Hide a dead welt with a patch.

Solution
Cover it up

Particularly when the welt is decidedly DOA, simply shroud the departed welt completely. Note that with the exception of plain patches and appliqués, you will still have access to the welts and pockets underneath these following rescues.

With a patch or appliqué

If your fabric has a busy pattern, you may be able to get away with a patch that blends in by carefully matching patterns and invisibly slipstitching the patch in place along its turned-under edges (see pp. 6-13 on applying patches and appliqués).

With a patch pocket

Cut a large enough patch pocket to cover the welt, and construct the pocket as usual. Place it over the welt to hide it completely.

"*I once made a black cotton pantsuit with double-welt pockets. The welts looked horrible and looked even worse every time I gently hand-washed the outfit. I am allergic to ironing, even though it would have helped. Instead of living with the puckers and wrinkles, I bypassed the problem by patching the welts closed with a piece of grosgrain ribbon zigzagged over them and then covering the area with a patch pocket. Nobody sticks their hands in my pockets but me.*"

With a flap

1 Cut a flap that is at least
½ in. longer than the botched
welt. The flap can be a simple
rectangle, or you can use a
shaped flap pattern piece from
another pattern and adjust the length to fit.

2 Construct the flap as usual, then baste the upper
edges together at the seamline. Trim the upper seam
allowance of the flap to ¼ in., and finish the upper
raw edge.

3 Center the flap about ¼ in. above the upper welt,
right sides together and upside down, so the finished
edge of the flap butts the upper welt seam.

4 Stitch the flap to the garment, beginning and ending
precisely at each end of the flap, along the basting.

5 Next, turn the flap down over the welt to cover it.
Press and secure the flap in place by topstitching along
its upper edge or by slipstitching the top ½ in. of the
sides of the flap to the garment.

> **TIP** When you sew down the flap to the garment, whether by hand or by machine, be sure to tuck the ends of the flap seam allowance under the flap so they will not show on the finished garment.

With a single welt

1 Construct a single welt as you would a flap. The welt
can be a basic rectangle or shaped, but it needs to be
bigger in length and width than the botched double or
single welts you wish to cover.

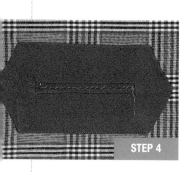

STEP 4

② Center the finished edge of the welt, right sides together and upside down, over the lower welt seamline.

③ Stitch in a ¼-in. seam, turn up the welt and press, then topstitch or slipstitch the ends to secure.

With another welt or set of welts

① With contrasting or self-fabric, make a new single or double welt the same size as the originals.

② Sew the welts onto the center of a piece of fabric cut to an attractive shape: geometric, free form, a print motif, and so on.

③ Apply the unit over the old welts, either as an appliqué with a zigzag or by turning under the raw edge and topstitching or slipstitching in place.

④ By hand, slipstitch the under and lower layers of welts together so that the under layer will not show on the finished garment.

With trim

Choose trim that is wide enough to cover the welts, such as braid, flat lace trim, or ribbon. Turn under the ends of the trim, and baste them over the welts to cover them. Stitch in place by hand or machine. The strips of trim should butt together in the center of a double welt.

This braid conceals a set of botched welts.

Solution
Disguise it

Many sewers will embellish anything that does not run away fast enough from us, so if you end up with puckers at the ends of welts, here's your chance to decorate them.

With buttons, beads, shells, and charms

Check your sewing or craft store or your button box for small, decorative doodads to sew over the puckered ends. Use the same object elsewhere on the garment for continuity.

With a hand-embroidered arrowhead

These are often seen on better designer garments because they increase durability and they are decorative. Use embroidery thread or silk buttonhole twist for the arrowhead.

For an industrial look

This is tough and edgy and says loudly, "Don't mess with me; I can wear my zippers however I please." Sew a heavy-duty metal or plastic sport zipper over the welt with the tapes showing on the right side of the garment. To do so, close the zipper, turn the ends of the zipper tape under, and baste the zipper to cover the welts. Stitch in place close to the zipper teeth and again close to the edge of the zipper tape. The tapes will cover the botched welts.

Buttons cover puckers at the ends of these welts.

Embroidered Arrowhead

Step 1
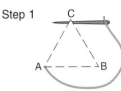

Step 2

Step 3

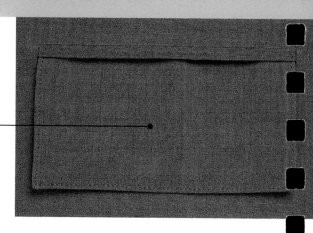

Fixing Flap Fatigue

Do you often find that your flaps are fading fast? Are they too short or too long to fit their welts? Do they look as if they have a bad case of a sartorial sickness of some kind? Fortunately, flap problems are nearly as easy to fix as flaps are to bungle.

Solution
For flaps that are too long

If the flaps are too long to fit into double welts, there will be unattractive puckering on the flap where it is attached under the upper welt. Here are some solutions.

TIP These techniques for fixing flaps work best for natural fibers. For synthetics, you may not be able to shrink or stretch the flap to fit precisely.

Easestitch by hand

Sew a small running stitch along the flap's upper seamline, pulling in the excess width so the flap fits the opening. Secure the gathering thread to the flap. Press the flap gently with steam over a ham to shrink out the excess width, then allow it to dry and cool thoroughly

on the ham before you pick it up (see the top photo at right). Insert the flap into the welt, again over a ham, and secure it in place by sewing the flap's upper seam allowance and upper welt seam allowance together by hand or machine (see the bottom photo at right).

All welt and flap applications, whether basting or pressing, should be performed on a tailor's ham. That is because the area of the body over which these design details typically fall is curved, not flat. Show me welts on a jacket that lie flat when the garment is on a hanger, and I'll show you welts that want to pull open when the garment is worn.

In natural fibers, you can shrink a flap to fit its welt.

Ready-to-Wear: The House of Pancakes

Generally, the ready-to-wear industry manufactures garments to look flat on a hanger because that looks tidy to consumers who quickly paw through racks of clothes as they shop. They call this phenomenon "hanger appeal." Flatness in garments requires less labor in terms of darts, shaped seams, and other construction that provides a precise and curvy fit. Also, more consumers can squeeze into what I affectionately call "pancake" garments because there is little exact fit built into the garment, which hangs on the body like a dust cover on a piece of furniture.

Note that really fine custom-tailored jackets look baggy and rumpled in odd places on the hanger or when laid flat. I once read an article on custom clothing in a major fashion magazine, which was illustrated with a photo of a custom jacket laid flat; it looked like such a crumpled mess that it must have broken its tailor's heart. If the jacket had been photographed on the lady for whom it had been made, however, it would have skimmed her body like Lycra.

So remember, if a garment lies flat on a hanger, it will not precisely fit your curves, but if it looks lumpy-dumpy on the hanger, it just might.

Solution
For flaps that are too short

I have a photo of a $5,490 jacket made out of white snakeskin by a famous Italian designer. The front of the jacket features four double-welt pockets with shaped flaps. Only one corner of the four flaps' sides properly covers the welts; the other seven corners reveal ½ in. to ¾ in. of the ends of the welts. For an extra dose of schadenfreude, you may delight in learning that the laps were uneven at the bottom of the jacket, the hem in general was lumpy and uneven, and the pocket and flap placement was not level from right to left. Your mistakes are much cheaper, right?

Stretch the flap

Use pins to stretch the flap over the curves of a ham. Press with steam, and allow the flap to cool and dry thoroughly.

Shrink the welts to fit the flap

1 Run a small, straight gathering stitch through the welts' seamlines, then pin or baste the ends of the flap to the ends of the welts.

2 Pull up the extra length in the welts to match the length of the flap, and secure the gathering stitch. Baste the flap by hand by sewing through the upper welt's seam ditch.

3 With the garment placed over a ham, gently press with steam to shrink out the extra width in the welts. Allow it to cool and dry before you remove it from the ham.

4 Next, sew the flap to the upper welt on the wrong side by hand or machine as usual.

STEP 5

5 Finally, invisibly tack down the upper $\frac{1}{8}$ in. of each end of the flap to the garment so that the ends of the welts will not show but the flap can still be worn either inside or outside of the pocket.

Decorate the gap

Sew on a decorative charm, button, appliqué, or other trim to cover the space between each end of the welts and the flaps.

Flipping, Flopping, Puckering, and Pulling

Welts and flaps aren't the only obstacles that can trip up sewers. Design details such as collars can curl and flip the wrong way, ribbing can look floppy, facings peek out where they do not belong, and seams pucker and pull. To treat your injured ego, try the following well-stocked first-aid kit of quick fixes.

Solution
If the collar at the center back rises above the neck seam

On jackets and shirts, this problem is caused by too little width at the lower curved edge of the collar at the center back.

For shawl collars

Let out the center-back collar seams at the lower edge. The extra width at the lower edge of the collar will allow it to fit the curves of the wearer's neck so it will not ride up.

Stretch the collar

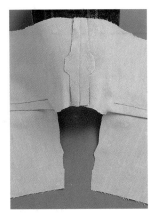

Place the collar over a ham and stretch the lower center-back edge of the collar with steam. Use pins inserted through the collar into the ham to secure it. Allow it to dry and cool before handling.

Tack by hand

This cure is really cheating, but only your dry cleaner will know. Use a tiny French tack to secure the under-side of the collar at the center back of the neck seam, about ½ in. from the finished lower edge. When worn, the tack should not show, nor should it cause any pull lines as the wearer moves.

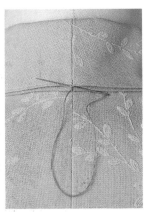

Solution
Curly collar corners

I see these frequently on shirts and jackets, particularly on ready-to-wear. Generally, the collar curls up because the upper collar is too small and the under collar is too big at the ends of the collars. If you have already trimmed and clipped before you discovered the curl, ripping and resewing will not do. Here are two cures for collar curls on completed garments.

Let out the center-back seam for shawl collars; if all else fails, tack the collar in place.

> **TIP** Before trying any other methods, **always try** pressing the collar right side up over a ham, using a press cloth and plenty of steam, to get the corners to curve down rather than up.

Curly collar corners can be straightened.

If you still have easy access to the inside of the collar, apply interfacing

This technique can help you with an unlined jacket that is merely slipstitched closed at the neck seams, for example.

1. Start by turning the collar wrong side out.

2. Cut a very stiff piece of interfacing to fit the last couple of inches of the collar's ends. This is often called a "quarter patch."

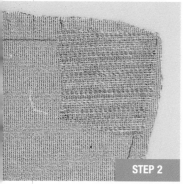

STEP 2

3. Catchstitch or fuse the interfacing to the underside of the collar, and stitch it through all layers to the collar points over the original stitching.

4. Trim, turn, and press right side up using a press cloth over a ham.

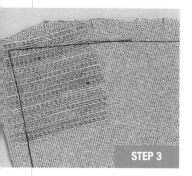

STEP 3

> **TIP**
>
> On men's dress shirts, a collar stay, which is a flat piece of plastic with one pointed end, is sewn into the underside of a collar's points to keep them looking sharp. Usually, the stays can be removed for laundering and pressing from the underside of the collar through a flap or a small buttonhole. Collar stays are typically available in the notions department of your sewing store.

Apply boning to the right side of the under collar

Boning will help on heavier fabrics, such as on wool jackets and coats. This technique is particularly useful on peaked lapels that won't lie flat.

1. Use a collar stay or cut a piece of lightweight plastic or spiral steel boning about ½ in. less than the distance from the collar's point diagonally to the upper edge. For

plastic boning, shape one end into a rounded point, and discard any fabric casing.

2 Cut a piece of bias-cut self-fabric, ribbon, twill tape, or other trim that is slightly wider than the boning to be used as a casing.

3 Place the boning diagonally from the point of the collar toward the neck, centering it over and at right angles to the curved area. Cover it with the casing material, and slipstitch in place. You can leave the top of the casing open to remove the boning for pressing if desired.

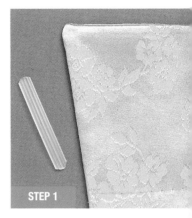

STEP 1

Solution
For wimpy ribbing

If the only ribbing that you can find to match your garment is the soft, floppy kind that doesn't hold its shape as a neckband or cuff, here are some solutions.

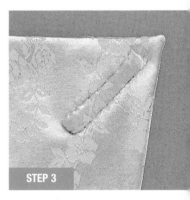

STEP 3

Insert elastic

1 Open up the inside area of the ribbing seam.

2 Cut a piece of elastic the same width as the ribbing.

3 Insert the elastic inside the ribbing, and secure the ends.

4 Slipstitch the ribbing closed. The elastic will stiffen the cuff or band but will allow for stretch.

STEP 4

Variations

- ◆ *If you find yourself stuck with floppy ribbing, try cutting the ribbing double.*

- ◆ *If you do not need much stretch in the ribbing, try using a fusible knit interfacing. Test the resulting degree of stretch on a scrap.*

- ◆ *Instead of ribbing, look for swimwear fabrics or other knits that stretch enough and that coordinate with your garment.*

Solution
If facings roll to the right side of a garment

Particularly if you are sewing synthetics, you can press until the cows come home, but facings may not stay put.

Particularly if you are sewing synthetics, you can press until the cows come home, but facings may not stay put.

Understitch by hand or machine

By hand for luxury garments, sew a tiny prick stitch from the facing side, catching the seam allowances only, close to the seam. Take care to not allow the stitches to show on the right side of the garment. To understitch a facing by machine, use a fairly short straight stitch with the right side of the facing up, and sew close to the facing seam while pushing the seam allowances underneath toward the facing.

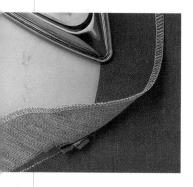

Understitch by machine, but use fusible thread in the bobbin. Press to favor the right side of the garment.

With fusible thread

Understitch by machine, but use fusible thread in the bobbin. Press to favor the right side of the garment.

Topstitch

Do you remember 1970s-style polyester, double-knit leisure suits? Nearly every edge had to be topstitched to hold its shape, since polys do not press. Topstitching helps prevent rolling, and it is decorative.

Topstitch edges to hold them in place.

Solution
Pleats and creases won't hold their shape

Perhaps because I learned to sew in the late 1960s on "permanent press" fabrics, which were formaldehyde-glazed, polyester shirtings that could have doubled for sheet metal in shop-class projects, I've learned a few tricks for keeping the sharp creases that were popular then and frequently become popular again.

For natural fibers

1 Baste the creases in place.

2 Using a utility sprayer, spray with a mixture of 50% water and 50% white vinegar. Test the water and vinegar solution on a scrap to ensure that it will not leave a mark. I have never had a problem with it.

3 Cover with a press cloth and press.

4 Allow the creases or pleats to dry thoroughly before moving them. Leave the basting in as long as possible during construction.

> **TIP** For pleated skirts, hem the skirt **before set-ting** the pleats whenever possible. If you have a press, setting pleats is one of its best uses. For a pleated skirt that is completely basted, press the creases from both the right side and the wrong side of the garment to set them thoroughly.

Topstitch the inside fold of pleats

Stitch close to the fold to hold the fold in place. If you don't mind the topstitching showing on the right side, you can topstitch both creases on pants and pleats on dresses and skirts close to the folds. This is not just a 1970s revival look but a practical way to hold the sharp shape of uniforms, athletic clothing such as pleated field hockey or golf skirts, and hard-wearing work clothes.

Insert fusible thread into the inside of the creases

This method is quite sneaky but fast and easy.

1 Set the creases or pleats by pressing, as described above.

2 Next, cut a length of fusible thread or ¼-in. fusible webbing the length of the crease.

3 Slip the fusible inside the crease, and position it right on the crease line. This will require some touchy-feely fiddling.

4 When you have it as close as possible to the inside of the crease, press it in place.

STEP 3

Solution
For roly-poly waistbands

Waistbands that roll over are unattractive and uncomfortable. When this happens, usually the band is too tight, but sometimes it may be simply too soft.

Enlarge the band

Let the band out as much as possible at the ends, replace it with a longer one cut from scraps, or replace it with a grosgrain ribbon waistband, as described on p. 28.

STEP 4

Stiffen the band

Without taking the skirt or pants apart, you can use grosgrain ribbon in a width slightly less than that of the waistband. Center the ribbon along the wrong side of the band, and turn the raw ends under. Either topstitch, slipstitch, or prickstitch the ribbon in place.

Grosgrain ribbon adds stiffness to a completed waistband.

Puckers at lapel and collar junctures are embarrassing.

Solution
Puckers and pull lines

Puckers and pull lines are a pox on perfection, but they happen. They are as common as pimples on teenagers. When they pop out, try the following poultices.

For puckers on coats and jackets at the lapel and collar junctures

These can ruin the look of a jacket, but they are so easy to avoid and to fix after the fact.

> **TIP** Do not try to overpress the pucker out or you may make matters worse by smashing your fabric's fibers beyond redemption. If you cannot gently steam and finger-press out the pucker, try the following rescues.

1 From the inside, check that the trimming and clipping is adequate, then check if you inadvertently caught the seam allowances of the collar or the lapels in the stitching where they join.

2 If so, release the stitches so the seam allowances at that juncture are free, then turn the garment right side out to check if the pucker has disappeared.

3 If not, turn the juncture wrong side out again, and carefully rip out the last few stitches of the facing/collar seam on either side of the neckline seam where the

To avoid a pucker altogether, remember to stop stitching ⅛ in. from the neckline seam, and resume about ⅛ in. on the other side of the lapel juncture. Do not catch any of the seam allowances in the stitching.

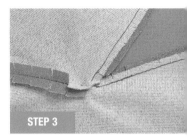

STEP 3

collar and lapels join. Leave the "hole" as is. It's not a stress point, so it will not get bigger with wear. The little hole will eliminate the pucker.

Pull lines and ripples on bias binding

1 Try seam pressing, very gently, with an up-and-down movement. Do not smash the binding with every ounce of your body weight; do not use your press; and do not drag the iron over the binding or you may stretch it into more ripples. Just steam it and pat it with your fingers to encourage the drag lines to go away. Bindings should generally look slightly rounded and puffy, not flat and crisp.

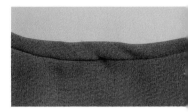

Pull lines on bindings
are a drag.

2 If pressing is not enough, then carefully remove the hand or machine stitches that secure the binding to the wrong side of the garment. Hold your iron over the binding and use steam only to relax it. While it cools and dries, give yourself a facial. Gently fold the binding back in place, coaxing it with your fingers into whatever curves are there, and slipstitch it in place on the wrong side of the garment.

If you prefer to machine-stitch the binding in place to the wrong side of the garment, try using fusible thread in the bobbin.

1 Machine-stitch along the foldline of the right side of the binding, turning under the raw edge with your fingers ("clean-finishing").

TIP

If you launder a bias-bound garment, you may need to press the binding each time you clean it to cure ripples, since warmth and water will relax the weave of the binding.

STEP 3

② Carefully ease the binding in place as described on p. 63, looking at the right side of the garment to make sure that the binding is an even width. Gently press it in place along the binding seamline, and avoid pressing the binding fold if possible.

③ Topstitch or ditchstitch the binding for extra durability.

Drag lines on topstitched seams

This very common problem is also caused by the action of a machine's feed dogs.

STEP 1

① Try pressing gently with steam. This will often eliminate drag lines, at least until you launder the garment.

② If that's not enough, rip out the topstitching in the rippled area, and pull the thread ends inside to secure.

③ Slip a piece of fusible web between the upper garment area and the lower seam allowances.

④ Press. This will stabilize the area so it will not shift as you sew.

⑤ Replace the topstitching, starting and ending at the old stitches and pulling the thread tails inside to secure.

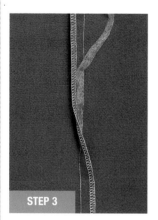

STEP 3

Alternative

Another option is to rip out the topstitching and retopstitch the seam through the upper layer of the garment only, leaving the seam allowances free. Use fusible thread in the bobbin. After top-stitching, press the seam gently to fuse it in place.

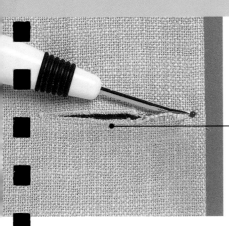

Bungled Buttonholes

Buttonholes are typically the last major hurdle that we jump over as we complete a garment. We are often tired and antsy by the time we get to them, so it's no wonder that they sometimes come out wrong. You needn't let a bad buttonhole deprive you of the pleasure of wearing your garment, however. Here are some solutions.

Solution
For severed bar tacks at the end of the buttonhole

It is so easy to slash through the bar tack or even through the garment when you open up buttonholes. To fix, mend the slash in the fabric as described in chapter 1. Then use trim, such as small appliqués, beads, brass charms, buttons, or points, on *all* of the buttonholes in the same manner.

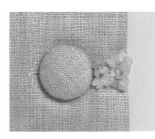

Beading conceals this overly slashed open buttonhole.

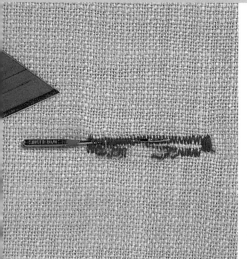

Solution
Rip and resew
an uncut buttonhole

This is for when you sewed it in the wrong place or if your machine malfunctioned. Ripping out a machine buttonhole is tremendously tedious, but it can be done. Put on your patience cap, and work from the back to avoid marring the right side of the garment. Using a small seam ripper, lift and cut the stitches, then use tweezers to pull out the threads. Also, you can reach inside between the front and front facing with a seam ripper to remove stitches.

> **TIP** When ripping out a buttonhole, try inserting a needle with great care under the row of satin stitches, then run a razor blade over the stitches on the needle to safely cut the threads. The needle will help protect the fabric underneath.

66 *A few years ago, I made a plaid wool coat dress for a customer. I matched those plaids to a fare-thee-well, the dress fit perfectly, and then I sewed the dozen or so little keyhole buttonholes that boldly marched up and down the center front of the dress.*

The circuit board on my electronic machine shorted out in the middle of the last buttonhole. I tried calling all over to find a sewer or a store with a machine that made a similar buttonhole but to no avail. Finally, I did my best to sew the rest of the botched buttonhole with another machine's satin stitch. I sure could tell the difference, but it really was hard to notice on the fuzzy and busy wool plaid. 99

Solution
If the buttonholes are too big

If the buttonholes are too big for the buttons or button-holes have stretched with wear, use a few small hand stitches on the wrong side of the buttonhole at each end to shorten the buttonhole.

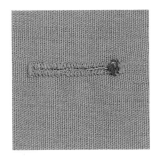

Contrast thread is shown for clarity.

Solution
For buttonholes on knits that look wobbly and rippled

Even when you carefully apply interfacing to the closure areas of knit garments, buttonholes will still often stretch and wobble, particularly over time, as the inter-facing softens with wear and cleaning. Here are some ways to fix that.

Rippled buttonholes are common on knits.

Cord them

From the wrong side, run a needle and doubled heavy thread, such as upholstery, quilting, embroidery, or buttonhole twist, under one row of satin stitches, leaving several inches of tail at the beginning. Next, turn the corner at the end of the buttonhole, and run the needle under the other side of the satin stitches. Secure the cording ends.

You can still cord a button-hole after it is stitched.

Use fusibles

Slip ¼-in. strips of fusible web or fusible interfacing (with the fusing agent toward the facing) between the front and the facing as close as possible to the buttonhole stitches. Gently pull the buttonhole out straight with your fingers to eliminate the ripples, or pin it straight on your ironing board. Press.

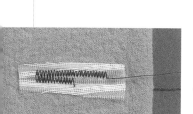

Restitch over a stabilizer. Contrast thread is shown for clarity.

Stiffen and overstitch

Place a piece of organza or a double layer of fine nylon net in a similar color on the underside of the buttonhole. Overstitch with a zigzag stitch along each side of the buttonhole. Alternately, you could overstitch by hand. Trim the stabilizer close to the stitching. This method works well on sheers, too.

> **TIP**
>
> If you have multiple buttonholes on a garment but have only botched one, you may need to "save" all of them so that they will all look the same.

Solution
Botched bound buttonholes

No matter how good yours are or how many times you've made them, bound buttonholes are fraught with peril. Like their larger cousins, double-welt pockets, bound buttonholes can come out with uneven lip widths, puckers, holes, and fraying at the ends, and they can wind up uneven in length with one another or unevenly spaced on the garment.

If there are puckers at the ends

Check that you have clipped closely enough, at a diagonal, from the center of the two rows of stitching to the ends of the stitching, like an "X" shape. Do not be afraid to clip right up to the ends of the stitches. If you sewed the short ends of the buttonhole in the shape of a rectangle, rip out the short ends of the stitching and leave it out. Overstitch the long ends for durability. Secure the triangles at the ends of the buttonhole with small hand or machine stitches as usual, and gently re-press. Often these measures will remove puckers at the ends.

If the fabric is closely woven and the area is stabilized with fusible interfacing

In this case, you can typically rip out the stitches that hold the welts in place and restitch them. You may also have to make the new bound buttonholes slightly longer and wider than the originals if the original stitching has marred the fabric.

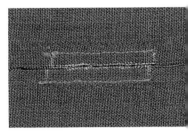

Restitch to correct.
Contrast thread is shown
for clarity.

> **TIP** Stitch bound buttonholes over a carefully positioned piece of graph paper for perfect size, position, and spacing. Pin the patches to the center front in the desired locations, and over those, pin a long strip of graph paper aligned to the edge of the garment. With a fine pencil or pen, use the graph paper to mark the sewing lines for all of the buttonholes, with whatever spacing, length, and distance from the edge you choose. Stitch over the marked lines, then tear away the paper.

Solution
DOA buttonholes

Sometimes buttonholes simply can't be saved, but we can bury them with dignity.

Cover them

Using a decorative fabric patch or a piece of trim as described on pp. 6-13, sew new buttonholes by machine over the patches. Alternately, sew the button on the overlap over the patches, and use another fastener between the top and bottom layers of the opening.

Cover the entire injured center front area

You could cover the area with a graft of trim a bit wider than the width of the buttonholes plus the distance between the buttonhole and the center front. Or you could sew on a reversed facing to look like a contrast band.

1 To add a reversed facing, cut a new facing out of matching or contrasting fabric, and press under the long, outside edges.

2 Sew the facing right side to the garment wrong side.

3 Trim, clip, turn, and press as usual. The facing will now be on the right side of the garment.

4 Topstitch or slipstitch the pressed-under edge to the garment.

5 To finish, either sew new buttonholes over the new trim or facing or use alternative fasteners such as snaps or hook-and-loop tape on the inside of the closure.

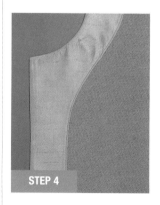

STEP 4

Mismatched Plaids and Patterns

I find little so irritating as when I carefully cut out a garment to match plaids and patterns, only to find that the matches are a bit off after I sew them.

Solution
If you are very close

If you are only a few threads off, stretch the two pieces in opposite directions at the seamlines, and press with steam and a press cloth while holding both sides of the seam in place with your fingers. If you topstitched both sides of the seam in opposite directions and the result was wavy gravy, this method can also help.

Sometimes slight mismatches can be steamed and stretched into position.

Solution
If you are not close enough

Even though it is common to see glaring mismatches in patterns on ready-to-wear (my "expensive mistakes" file is full of them), we home sewers can do it better. If you want to wear cheap-looking clothes, buy them. If you want quality clothes, make them.

It's easier to see the pattern matches from the garment right side.

Rip and resew

Either use lots of pins, sewing over them gently, slowly, and carefully by advancing the needle with the hand-wheel as you run over the pins, or baste by hand or by machine. Check the matches before sewing the seam permanently.

Use fusibles to help you match the patterns at the seam

After ripping, press the seam allowance of one side of the seam to the wrong side. With fusible thread in the bobbin, baste wrong side up, just inside the foldline and through the seam allowance only. From the right side, position the basted, folded edge with the fusible stitches down over the other seamline, match the patterns, and press. Gently open up the seam and stitch it permanently, close to the basting.

Solution
Distract from mismatches

Stitch rows of topstitching or decorative stitching over the seamline or on both sides of it. Or you could stitch trim over the seam. Think of a pair of black and white houndstooth check pants with a black satin or grosgrain ribbon running down the outseams.

Solution
For small garment pieces

For small garment pieces on plaids and stripes, such as pockets, collars, welts, yokes, flaps, facings, and cuffs, cut these pieces on the bias if you have the fabric. This avoids the matching issue altogether and adds to the design.

> **TIP** If you use the method of cutting small garment pieces on the bias, remember to cut the pieces so they match each other perfectly from left to right on the garment.

4

FITTING FLAWS

O f course we sewers all love a perfect fit, and we are all inordinately fond of the "P" word in general. Yet we all have only 24 hours in each of our busy days, we're human and we make mistakes, and we run out of time and take sewing "shortcuts" that we often later regret. If you want to actually wear the clothes you make, you can either try to keep your pride intact by giving your sewing mistakes to charity so at least you don't have to look at them any more, or you can subjugate that pride with your creative powers.

If Perfection, and I do mean that with a capital "P," is all that makes you happy, this book won't help you. If you can recognize your sewing mistakes as an opportunity to learn, to explore new design ideas, and to make the best of a difficult situation, then you can keep your pride and the garment, too. Here are some quick fixes for after-the-fact fitting failures.

what's inside

Too Short

Too Tight

Too Wide

Too Low Cut

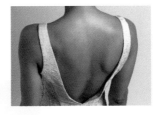

Gapping Necklines

Not Enough Ease

The Sleeve Doesn't
Fit the Armscye

"Recently, I made a rosy plum baby corduroy tunic that had contrast bands in a black with matching plum printed rayon at the lower sleeve, the hem, and a little bias binding at the neck. Since it was from a plus-size pattern, I 'knew' it would be big enough.

Of course it was a bit snug, and the plain expanse of unbroken color across my front made me look like Barney the dinosaur: large and purple. To fix it, I split the entire tunic, right down the center front and added vertical contrast bands and a row of buttons and buttonholes. The band not only added the 2 in. I needed in width but also added three sets of slenderizing vertical lines. This fitting failure encouraged me to improve the design of the tunic, so I'm much better off now than if I had not made a mistake in the first place!"

Too Short

When you find that your tops, pants, skirts, and sleeves come out too short, here are some grafting techniques that can bring them back to life.

TIP You can use all of the fitting treatments in this chapter to improve your ready-to-wear clothing, too. Often, changing the fit of a garment also changes its design and its function. When you lengthen that itty-bitty miniskirt so you can wear it to the office, you can get more use out of it. When you add Lycra gussets to that sexy but skin-tight jumpsuit that you only wore for parties, you'll find yourself knocking comfortably but stylishly around the house in it. When you add an elastic casing to the waist area of a voluminous chemise, you may reveal curves that you want to show off instead of hide.

Solution
Contrast bands

If you can sew a waistband, you can sew a contrast band.

1 Start by measuring how much extra garment length you need, then double this number and add the width of two seam allowances. For a 3-in. finished band, for example, you need the unfinished band to measure (3 in. x 2) + ($\frac{5}{8}$ in. x 2) = 7$\frac{1}{4}$ in.

wide. For the length of the band, measure the length of the lower edge of the garment you are treating, and add seam allowances if needed to match seams on the garment.

2 If the band will be circular, as for a contrast hem band, join the short ends of the piece in a ⅝-in. seam, trim the seam allowances by one-half, and press them open.

3 Sew one long side of the band, right sides together, to the lower edge of the garment.

4 Trim the seam and press it toward the band. For a shaped band, such as on a flared skirt, clip the seam to release the curves.

5 Fold the band in half lengthwise, then examine the band from the right side of the garment: It should be perfectly even in width all around the lower edge that you are lengthening. Adjust if necessary.

6 Pin the band in place along the upper edge, then press it lightly along the fold.

7 To complete, finish the remaining raw edge of the band and stitch-in-the-ditch from the right side to enclose the seam allowances and to secure the contrast band. On finer garments, turn under the seam allowance and slipstitch or prickstitch the band in place from the wrong side.

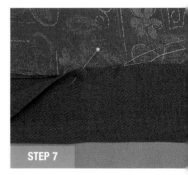

STEP 7

Contrast bands can be cut from the lengthwise grain, crossgrain, or bias. If you have enough fabric, bias bands drape beautifully. Take care, however, to avoid diagonal stress lines as you fold the band under to the wrong side of the garment. Work from the outside of the garment, lay the area over your ironing board, measure to keep the foldline and seamline parallel, and gently smooth out the band with your fingers. Press the band lightly to set the foldline, and pin it in place from the right side.

When possible, match the grain direction of the garment itself with the grain of the band. Which grain direction you actually choose will probably be determined by how much fabric you have to work with.

TIP If your fabric is lightweight, **you may want to interface contrast bands cut on the lengthwise grain or crossgrain for extra crispness.**

Solution
Self-fabric band

To make a self-fabric band, follow the steps for a contrast band but use matching fabric. If you do not like the look of the resulting seamline, you can distract from it by adding trim or topstitching. Try centering lace, ribbon, braid, or other decorative trim to cover up the seamline: Stand back from the garment and see if you like the look. If so, simply machine- or hand-stitch the trim in place. Or try using a decorative thread and machine embroidery right over the seamline to cover and distract from it. You could also topstitch by using a straight stitch on one or both sides of the seamline. Note that adding trim or topstitching often makes the seam look even more as if it were a planned part of the design than if you had left the seam plain.

Solution
Trim

Trim will cover a multitude of evils, and it will lengthen a multitude of shortcomings. The popularity of trim on garments waxes and wanes with the fashion market, but right now, it is very in, particularly among teenagers. Remember that flower-embroidered ribbon that you sewed onto the hems of your bell-bottomed, button-fly jeans back in the '70s? It's back! Now, teens can buy high-water jeans already embellished with happy hippie ribbon, which is lucky, because few of them would conceive of doing it themselves. Can macramé be far behind?

You can use one wide piece of trim to get the extra length you want, or you can sew together several strips of trim for the width you desire. Finish the raw edge of the garment, lap the trim over that finished edge, and topstitch by machine or slipstitch in place by hand. Any combination of plain or embellished ribbons, fringe, lace insertion, or even some upholstery trims will add length exactly where you need it.

Trims adds length where you need it.

> **TIP** Remember to match the care requirements for your trim to the care requirements for your garment. Always preshrink washable trim. To do so, loosely loop the trim into a circle, soak it in very warm water for about 20 minutes, lay the trim on a towel and roll up the towel to blot excess water, then hang the trim to dry thoroughly. Use your fingers to smooth and shape the trim if needed as you hang it to dry.

Solution
Mock cuffs

To lengthen pants, shorts, and sleeves, you can add a mock cuff if you have enough leftover fabric.

STEP 3

1 Cut the cuff from matching or contrasting fabric as for a contrast band. The length of the band should be equal to the circumference of the garment edge plus two seam allowances. To form a cuff, you will fold the band up onto itself, so cut the width of the band four times the desired finished measurement that you want to add to the sleeve or pants leg, plus two seam allowances. For example, for a finished cuff that would add 2 in. in garment length, you would need (2 in. x 4) + (⅝ in. x 2) = 9¼ in.

2 Attach the cuff just as for a contrast band, then fold the cuff up.

3 Tack the cuffs to the cuff seam at the inseams and outseams, just below the top foldline of the cuffs. On the right side of the garment, the seamline will hide inside the cuff's fold and will be indistinguishable from an attached cuff.

Too Tight

There is nothing less attractive and more uncomfortable than a garment that is too tight. Letting out the seam allowances is often not enough. Instead of committing the outfit to the back of your closet, try reviving it by using one of the following solutions.

Solution
Gussets

Gussets are simply rectangular, triangular, diamond-shaped, or football-shaped pieces of fabric that are inserted into a seam to produce more width. The location on a garment where you need extra width dictates the shape of the gusset. For example, to enlarge a wedding gown bodice, you might use the following shapes of gussets at the side seams with these corresponding results:

◆ A football-shaped gusset to enlarge mostly at the bust.

◆ A rectangular gusset to enlarge evenly the width along the side seams and the front and back armscye.

◆ A rectangular gusset that tapers to a point at the top of the side seam to enlarge the width at the side seams without enlarging the front and back armscye.

**Football-
Shaped
Gusset**

**Rectangular
Gusset**

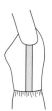

◆ A rectangular gusset topped with a cut-on triangle to enlarge the width at the side seams and at the front and back armscye.

◆ A diamond-shaped gusset at the upper sleeve and side seam to enlarge the armscye circumference.

Here's the basic method for applying a gusset.

**Tapered
Rectangular
Gusset**

① Start by carefully ripping out the seams that are too tight.

② Try the garment on, and measure the widest gap in the seams. Note the location and shape of that gap, and match it to the shape of your gusset.

③ Next, cut out the gusset, adding a generous seam allowance all around.

**Rectangular
Gusset with
a Cut-On
Triangle**

④ Sew the gusset to the garment seams, right sides together, breaking the thread at any points.

⑤ Trim, finish, and press the seam toward the garment.

**Diamond-
Shaped
Gusset**

Variations

STEP 5

Gussets are typically made from matching fabric, but you could also use contrasting fabric and use the colors of that contrast elsewhere on the garment to add to the design. For example, if you have made solid-colored pants to go with a printed top that came out too tight, you could use the solid color for gussets and pick up that color in buttons or other trim.

For active sportswear, use stretch fabrics for gussets. Remember to preshrink gusset fabrics and match care requirements to your garment.

Solution
Insert trim

The width of the trim that you choose will determine the width that you can add to the garment. Think of black wool crepe pants let out with wide black satin ribbon for a tuxedo effect. Try lace insertion to let out the princess seams on a cream silk blouse for a sexy but Victorian look. Simply rip out the too-tight seam, lap the trim just over the finished seam allowances, and topstitch in place.

Add width with decorative trim or with a strapped seam.

Solution
Add slits or vents

Adding slits or vents at lower side seams, princess seams, and center-back seams allows for extra width at the hips. For a slit, rip out the stitches from the lower edge of the garment to just below the waist, turn the seam allowances to the inside of the garment, and press. Topstitch or hemstitch in place.

For a vent, cut two rectangular extensions the length of the opening and about 3 in. wide.

1 Sew each extension to the length of each edge of the opened seam, grade the seams, and press both of the extensions along the seamlines toward the left side of the garment.

2 Finish the raw long edges that remain.

3 Topstitch through all layers at the top of the vent to secure, or on finer garments, catchstitch invisibly to the garment at the top of the vent.

Adding a Vent
Step 1

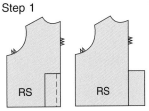

Add vent extensions.

Step 2

Sew the backs at the center-back seam, pivot, and sew across the top of the extension.

Step 3

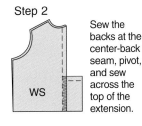

Catchstitch at the top of the vent.

Solution
Make a strapped seam

For a strapped seam, use strips cut on the lengthwise grain of self-fabric, contrast, or wide trim as an underlay.

1 Press under ¼ in. along the length of each finished seam allowance that you want to let out.

2 Slip the fabric strip (with raw edges finished) or trim underneath the seam allowances, and spread the seam the amount of the increase that you require. Take care to keep the two foldlines parallel.

3 Topstitch close to the folded edges.

Solution
Add a vertical contrast band to a center-front or center-back closure

When all you need to sneak in is a few extra inches in circumference, follow the instructions on pp. 76-78 for a horizontal contrast band, but cut the band on the lengthwise grain, interface it, and apply it to a center-front or center-back closure. Note that for a vertical band, you will need to sew up the ends of the band as you would for a waistband. Also, note that a vertical band will increase width at the neckline, so decide whether or not you'll like the extra width. On jewel necklines, for example, bodices that need extra width through the torso typically need extra width in the neck, too. On the other hand, wide, scooped necklines may become too wide if spread.

Too Wide

Sometimes when garments come out too big and we are too tired or rushed to refit and resew, the following methods of excessive width management can save the patient.

Solution
Darts

Sew one or a series of darts to the area that needs to be taken in. For example, you may want to add some at the waist of a chemise or at a skirt hem to peg it. Just try on the garment or put it on a dress form, wrong side out if your figure is fairly symmetrical, and pin as many darts of whatever depth and length that will take up the width that you want to eliminate. Don't try to calculate the dimensions mathematically or you are likely to make the garment too tight. Also, remember to allow for wearing ease. Be sure that the shape, dimensions, and positions of the darts are the same on the right and left sides of the garment.

Variations

For a sporty and edgy innie-outie look, sew the darts so they show on the right side of the garment. Think of tapering a short denim skirt hem with a series of shallow darts sewn on the right side in contrasting thread.

Vertical tucks can take up extra width in a decorative manner.

Solution
Vertical tucks

Fit the garment as described on p. 85, but sew as many tucks as you need to take up the extra width. As for darts, you can space tucks evenly around the circumference of the garment, or you can cluster them below the shoulder blades and bust apexes, where they will serve as conventional dart equivalents.

Variations

- *Tucks can also be sewn inverted so that the folds of extra fabric are on the inside of the garment. On the outside, you will see a row of parallel seams with each tuck released at each end. This kind of tuck is more tailored and tidy looking, since the excess fabric does not show on the right side.*

- *The folds of extra fabric can be pressed to one side or for wider tucks, pressed centered over the tuck's stitching.*

- *For tucks on striped fabric, try tucking the width of each stripe so only one color shows on the right side for an eye-catching effect.*

- *Secure tucks at the ends with buttons or other trim, or use decorative thread to sew the tucks.*

- *Use a double needle and a straight stitch to sew rows of closely spaced pin tucks over an area that needs to be taken in. To do so, you may need to loosen the needle tension until the tuck "pops" up. The resulting area will look somewhat like matching ribbing and will have some stretch.*

Solution
Easy elastic smocking

This is a cute, feminine, and casual look. Try it on sleeve edges, waistlines, or over any area where you want the look of a close fit but want to keep ease of movement. Elastic smocking is especially pretty on small to medium prints, since the ruched fabric forms another pattern as well as adds texture to your design.

① To smock, wind a bobbin by hand with elastic thread. Note that your machine may have a special thread guide for use with thick, decorative threads in the bobbin; if not, bypass the tension slots on the bobbin case.

② Sew evenly spaced rows with large stitches, stretching the fabric flat as you sew. When released, the fabric will pucker up and look smocked.

Make a test sample on a scrap to get a feel for how taut to hold the fabric in front of and behind the needle, how long a stitch length to use, and how closely to space the rows of stitches. In general, the lighter and thinner the fabric, the closer the rows and the shorter the stitch length should be.

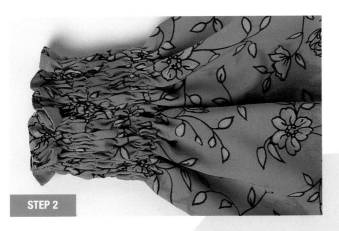

STEP 2

Too Low Cut

If you find yourself attracted to low necklines on an idealized pattern illustration or photo but feel a little overly breezy when you wear a low-necked garment, here are some easy "fill-ins" that will enhance your emotional comfort. If a neckline comes out too low for decency or your taste, rescue it as follows.

Solution
Lift at the shoulder seams

Rip out the shoulder seams, try the garment on, and lift either the front of the garment or the front and the back to raise the neckline. You can taper the width to the shoulder tip, or take it in all along the length of the shoulder seam, depending on your shoulder slope. Be sure to check the resulting fit at the underarm, bust, and sleeve cap. With this method, you may have to reposition bust darts or shorten the height of the sleeve cap correspondingly.

TIP

Since Misses patterns are drafted for fairly tall women, there is often too much length for many of us between the shoulder seams and bust. You can adjust the pattern on the front, back, and sleeve cap by pleating out that extra length, or you can take a deeper seam at the shoulder.

Solution
Horizontal tucks

As described, make tucks or a series of tucks across the front, back, and sleeve cap to take up extra length in a neckline. To add to the design, try using decorative thread or tucking the width of one color on a horizontal stripe. Baste the tucks in place, and try the garment on to ensure that the lower armscye and darts are in the right places. Note that horizontal tucks at the shoulders are slenderizing, since horizontal lines placed at the shoulders emphasize their width, which makes the waist and hips look smaller in comparison.

Remove extra length decoratively with tucks.

Solution
Modesty panel

For garments without a closure at the center front, fill in a neckline with a modesty panel. These aren't called dickies any more, you'll be happy to know. Modesty panels are big time-savers: It takes far less time to whip up a modesty panel than it does to sew a blouse.

Sewn in

1 Cut two pieces of matching or contrast fabric in whatever shape corresponds to the neckline, and add a ⅝-in. seam allowance to the top of the panel plus a 1½-in. margin around the other edges.

2 Sew the two pieces right sides together at the upper edge, grade the seam, turn it right side out, under-stitch, and press.

③ Finish the raw edges of the modesty panel.

④ Next, slip the panel into the neckline, and pin it in place. Either machine-stitch the panel to the garment facing only from the inside of the garment and topstitch around the neckline through the panel to secure it, or catchstitch the panel in place by hand on the inside.

Snapped in

Alternately, to fill a neckline with a closure at the center front, use snaps or hook-and-loop tape to secure the panel temporarily to the inside of the neckline.

Pinned to bra straps

This is one good use for your grandmother's old lace-edged doilies or hankies, small scarves folded in half diagonally, or other pieces of decorative fabric or wide trim. Instead of securing the modesty panel to the garment, simply safety-pin the folded or trimmed edge to your bra straps where they attach to the cups. Could this be easier?

You can add a small, flat weight to the bottom of the panel to discourage it from escaping the neckline and flapping in the breeze, or just tuck the lower edge of the panel under the lower edge of your bra.

> **TIP** Modesty panels that are snapped or pinned in may allow you to wear a jacket without a blouse underneath, which also helps prevent heat exhaustion in warm and humid climates.

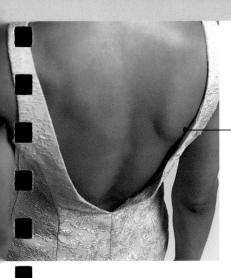

Gapping Necklines

Necklines can gap away from the body for many reasons. Sometimes they stretch during construction; sometimes we have concave curves on our bodies under necklines where others might have convex curves; and sometimes necklines swoop to precarious depths that simply must be stayed to preserve public decency, whether or not you are a Hollywood starlet sashaying into an awards ceremony. Spirit gum might fail you. If your neckline is bulging out of place, perform some simple surgery to fix it.

Solution
Take in the shoulder seams

Take in the shoulder seams as described on p. 88 on the front of the garment only. Often this is enough to move the neckline up from a concave area of the chest to a convex area and eliminate the gapping.

Solution
Stay the neckline

A stay is any device that helps hold a garment to your body or that helps hold a particular style as designed. If you have already finished the neckline with a facing or binding, try the following stays.

Stay tape

1 Sew a row of basting by machine or hand through all the layers of the neckline.

2 Pull up a thread to tighten the neckline, and secure it to a pin by twisting it around the pin in a figure eight.

3 To check for gapping, try on the garment, and adjust the basting so there are as few gathers as possible.

4 On the wrong side, sew a narrow strip of twill tape, selvage, ribbon, or other similarly narrow and non-stretchy material over the basting by hand along both long edges of the stay with a felling stitch.

5 By machine, topstitch through all layers.

6 To finish, lay the neckline over a ham, and from the right side, use steam only and gentle pats from your fingers to shrink the neckline to the stay and eliminate any puckers. This method works best with natural fibers and for necklines with up to about 1 in. of gap.

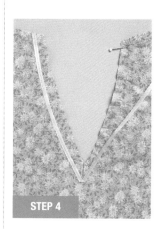

STEP 4

TIP How much puckering and gathering at the neckline you are willing to tolerate is a matter of taste and design. Since I make nearly all of my own clothes, it is a sheer pleasure for me to buy a cheap nightgown from a catalog. Invariably, since ready-to-wear manufacturers assume that all plus-size women are tall, wide at the shoulders, and big busted, and I'm none of the above, the necklines are ridiculously wide and deep. To remedy this, I topstitch through the gown and the neck facing to form a casing for elastic. I may also stitch the elastic directly to the neckline with a multiple zigzag or zigzag, stretching the elastic as I sew.

Variations

◆ If you don't want the elastic to show on the inside of the garment, sew topstitching around the neckline a distance from the finished edge that is slightly greater than the width of the elastic. Use a seam ripper to open up one shoulder seam between the topstitching and the finished neckline edge only, then insert elastic as if it were a casing.

◆ If the neckline is finished with a binding, try opening up the binding seam on the inside and pulling an appropriate width of elastic through the binding as if for a casing.

◆ You can insert narrow ribbon and bias tubing into a topstitched casing with the seam opening on the right side of the garment for a casual, peasant-blouse look.

Elastic stay

Apply narrow elastic as you would rigid stay tape. This works well with nonnatural fibers that will not shrink into place, such as nylon and polyester. Clear elastic works well because it is not bulky and its transparency makes the stay blend into the neckline finish.

An inverted pleat tightens up a neckline.

"Once when my two children were small, I was awakened in the wee hours by loud noises of yelling, fighting, and general mayhem. I leaped from bed to break up the fight and gave them my typical loud, long lecture about 'it's okay to play quietly when the old fogies are asleep, but it's NOT okay to wake us up!' Instead of denying, arguing, or ignoring me as usual, they acted positively gob smacked: speechless, sputtering, flapping their gums soundlessly like fish out of water.

Finally, I realized that half of my bust was hanging out of the overly large and droopy neckline of my purchased nightgown, as if I were some very angry, avenging warrior goddess prepared to unleash her sword upon them. Well, that quieted them down for a while. Now I stay my necklines."

Solution
Add darts, tucks, or pleats

Try on the garment, then pinch out as many darts, tucks, or pleats as you need through all layers to cure the gapping. You might use one large, inverted pleat at the center back, for example, if you want to tighten up the back neckline without reducing width across the rest of the back, or try a series of pin tucks radiating out from a circular neckline for a decorative effect.

The folds of excess fabric can be placed on the inside or outside of the garment. After stitching, press the folds to one side or center the fold over the stitches, then secure the extra fabric to the finished neckline with slip-stitches so they do not show on the right side.

"Do not laugh about this dart idea. I have a magazine photo of a pricey, designer evening gown that uses four vertical waist darts to snug the extremely low back of the gown to the model's back. It also features four horizontal darts radiating from the center-back seam, below the fanny, to closely fit and accent the derriere. We know what to call these, don't we?

If you don't like the appearance of these darts, consider covering them up with trim, appliqués, or other embellishments, such as rhinestone neckline clips."

Solution
Make a boning finger

In my custom-dressmaking business, I often make wedding dresses with extremely low necklines in front, back, and sometimes both in the front and back of the gown. I have often wished I could simply trail around after my client like a conjoined twin, with one finger gently and discreetly holding a gap to the curve of the body between the breasts or to the small of the back. Well, I'd have to make a matching outfit for myself to get away with that, and the bride (and the groom, for that matter) might not be interested in that much togetherness, so I figured out how to make a prosthesis for just that purpose.

① To make a boning finger, cut a finger-length piece of plastic or spiral-steel boning, round or cap the ends, and discard any casing.

② From matching fabric, sew a narrow tube the length of the boning plus about 1½ in., sewing across one short end. Turn the tube right side out.

③ Insert the boning, turn under the upper raw edge about ¼ in. from the end of the boning, and slipstitch the tube closed.

④ Slipstitch the upper edge of the covered finger to the inside of the garment at the location of the gap so that it will lift up like a hinge and will not show when worn.

To use the finger, just stick it underneath the wearer's bra band or panty elastic. The boning is thin enough so that the wearer will not be conscious of it, and the boning and hinge will flex sufficiently to allow for body movement without gapping.

STEP 4

—Not Enough Ease

Even when garments fit well by conventional standards, you may find after living in them a while that recommended wearing and design ease are inadequate to allow for active movement. For clothes designed for those who like to lift, reach, stretch, stride, and bend vigorously without restriction, for athletes and performers, and for plus-size women whose bodies are soft and compressible, here are some ways to increase ease specifically for active movement.

Solution
Godets

Like their close cousins, gussets, godets are simply triangular pieces of fabric, contrasting or matching, that are inserted into the lower edge of a seam to increase width at the hem for movement.

To insert a godet into a seam

1. Rip out the seam to the length that you would like the finished gusset. For example, for a mid-calf-length skirt or pants, you might want to rip below the knee level; for a long sleeve, rip midway between the elbow and wrist; and for a long evening dress, rip from mid-calf.

2. Reinforce the upper end of the ripped seam by using small pieces of fusible interfacing and over-stitching.

3 Next, cut the godet in a triangular shape that is the length of the opened seam, adding a ⅝-in. seam allowance at the point of the triangle plus a hem allowance on the lower edge. If the godet is wider than about 4 in. at its base, you need to curve the lower edge slightly to match the curve of the garment's hemline, or it will end up looking like the outside edge of a very old nickel.

4 Sew the godet to the garment with right sides together, breaking the thread at the upper point.

5 Press the seam allowances toward the garment.

To insert a godet where there is no seam

This may sound complicated but it isn't. There isn't any seam to rip out, and there is only one extra step to reinforce the point of the godet.

1 Start by drawing a vertical line on the wrong side of your garment where you wish to insert a godet.

2 To reinforce the upper point, center a 1-in. circle of fusible interfacing over the top of the line on the wrong side of the garment, and fuse it in place. Then place another circle of matching fabric over the location of the point on the right side.

3 Sew small machine stitches ¼ in. from both sides of this line, tapering to and pivoting at the point, through the interfacing and the fabric circle. Then slash along the line closely up to but not through the point.

4 Turn the fabric circle to the inside and press. This creates a little facing for the point, and it reinforces the area.

STEP 2

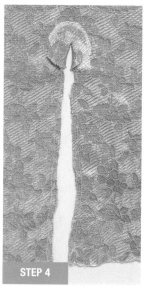

STEP 4

5 Next, cut a godet to fit and insert it as explained above, stitching it in place just outside of the reinforcement stitching. Break the stitching about ⅛ in. before the point; that little "hole" will help avoid a pucker at the top of the godet.

6 Press the seams toward the garment.

STEP 6

Variations

Godets are curvy, swingy, and feminine. Contrast godets add greatly to a garment's design as well as allow for movement. Think of lace godets revealing a bit of leg beneath a dance skirt, for example, or hot-pink satin godets flashing at the hemline of a long, straight black satin evening gown.

Solution
Pleated underlay

This is a cross between a godet, a gusset, a vent, and an inverted pleat. You can use matching or contrasting fabric.

1 Rip out the seam as for a godet, and reinforce the end of the stitching.

2 Cut a rectangle of fabric the length of the insert plus a ⅝-in. seam allowance at the top and a hem allowance at the lower edge. The width of the piece should be two times the finished width of the pleat plus two seam allowances. For exam-

ple, for a 2-in.-wide finished pleated underlay, the width of the fabric piece should be (2 in. x 2) + (⅝ in. x 2) = 5¼ in. wide.

③ Sew the long edges of the insert to the opened-up seam, and press the seam allowances toward the garment.

④ To finish the pleat, mark the center of the underlay between the two seams. Then position that mark at the top of the opening of the seam so that the underlay forms a box pleat on the inside of the garment and an inverted pleat on the right side.

⑤ To press from the right side, close the original seam with your fingers, baste in place if necessary, and arrange the underlay equally on each side of the seam. Press to set the pleat.

⑥ Secure the upper edge of the pleat with machine top-stitching or catchstitch by hand.

Solution
Stretch gussets

To apply stretch gussets for active movement, see pp. 81-82. Think of a quilted ski bib with a contrasting Lycra gusset running up the side seams like a racing stripe, or air-conditioned stretch lace gussets under the close-fitting arms of a dress or blouse to dance in.

The Sleeve Doesn't Fit the Armscye

As we sewers struggle to get a garment to fit our bodies, it's sometimes easy to forget that all the pieces of a garment have to fit each other, too. The armscye is a complicated place where this problem frequently occurs. For fitted, set-in sleeves that do not fit into the garment properly, try the following rescues.

Solution
If the length of the sleeve cap is too long

If the length is too long, the sleeve cap puckers or is difficult to ease into the armscye. To fix, rip out the armscye seam from notch to notch, and take a slightly deeper seam on the sleeve only. Alternately, take up the extra width at the sleeve cap with decorative gathers, darts, or tucks.

Darts reduce the length of a sleeve cap.

Solution
If the length of the sleeve cap is too short

If the length is too short, the sleeve may have required little or no easing into the armscye from notch to notch. This may cause pull lines across the upper arm and restriction of arm movement. To correct, remove the sleeve from the armscye.

Take in the armscye at the shoulder and upper side seams

Take in the armscye as fit allows to reduce its circumference. You can also add armscye darts, front and/or back, as needed for fit. Then set in the sleeve.

Enlarge the sleeve cap

You can enlarge the sleeve cap by using matching or contrast gussets, trim insertions, decorative slits, or peekaboo appliqués as described on pp. 12-13.

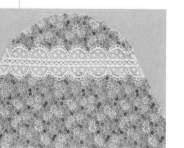

Lace insertion adds needed length to this sleeve cap.

TIP

In general, in the best of all possible worlds, if the sleeve fits the arm and the armscye fits the body, then they ought to fit together. During a fitting, don't hesitate to try combinations of darts, tucks, or gathers in various places on the armscye and on the sleeve cap to get both pieces to fit you and to fit together. This is the creative part!

For Sleeves, Yesterday's "Fit" Might Be Tomorrow's Failure

Bear in mind that fashion influences the way we perceive and judge good fit, and both fashion and our values change over time. For example, those of us who sewed during the '70s or earlier learned to desire a set-in sleeve that was quite different from those we see today. On a natural or cut-in shoulder for a bodice, we looked for an armscye that lay fairly close to the body and high under the arm; this type of sleeve reveals the shape of the body and allows for greater arm movement than does a more loosely set-in sleeve. In the '80s, on the other hand, we became accustomed to an extended-shoulder sleeve style that was looser by design, was supported by a substantial shoulder pad, and was meant to skim and drape over rather than precisely fit the shoulder area.

More recently, the ready-to-wear industry has reduced labor and fabric requirements by drafting sleeve caps that are relatively short and narrow so that they require little easing. This very commonly worn style of sleeve tends to restrict arm movement and to throw horizontal lines from notch to notch across the sleeve cap. Look around the next time you're in a crowd of people for this type of sleeve; only sewers would complain about the fit. Remember that the style of the sleeve that you want for your garment influences how precise a fit is desirable.

Variations

At an educational conference of the Professional Association of Custom Clothiers, I had the pleasure of meeting a famous and talented husband and wife design team from New York. The wife was wearing a simple dress with short zippers inserted into the top of the armscye seams. She wore them open to reveal a flash of shoulder, which looked unexpected and adorable. Try inserting zippers the next time your sleeve cap circumference is too short; the resulting gap when the zippers are open will allow for a comfortable fit.

Solution
If the shoulder seam is too long

Set-in sleeves will fall off the shoulder if the shoulder seam is too long. If you don't want to reset the sleeve or add a larger and wider shoulder pad, here are some sneaky cures.

Use one or more tucks or darts

Use tucks or darts on the inside or outside of the garment, from the upper chest level and from front to back, right through the shoulder seam. One wide tuck can be positioned at the end of the shoulder to form a flange, or a series of darts or tucks can be centered on the seam.

Gather the shoulder seam or add a casing

Rip out the shoulder seam, gather each edge, and resew to the shoulder length you desire for a shirred, casual look. You could also sew close to both of the pressed-open, finished edges of the shoulder seam to form a casing on each side of the seam. Then insert a narrow bias tube or ribbon, and pull up the drawstring to fit your shoulder length. Tie the drawstring in a bow at the shoulder edge or the neckline edge of the garment.

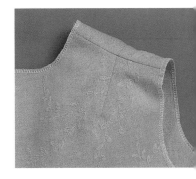

Darts through the shoulder seam can eliminate excess length.

Stitch through the shoulder seam allowances to form a casing to take up extra length.

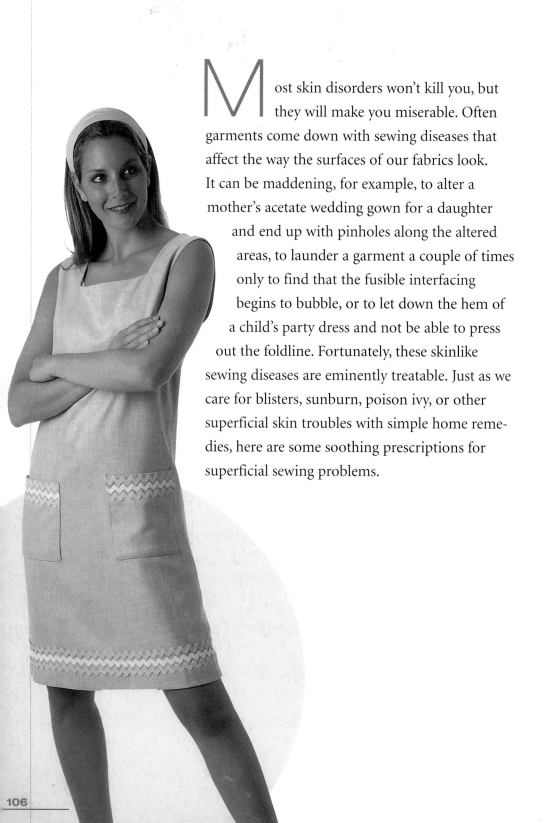

5
SURFACE PROBLEMS

Most skin disorders won't kill you, but they will make you miserable. Often garments come down with sewing diseases that affect the way the surfaces of our fabrics look. It can be maddening, for example, to alter a mother's acetate wedding gown for a daughter and end up with pinholes along the altered areas, to launder a garment a couple of times only to find that the fusible interfacing begins to bubble, or to let down the hem of a child's party dress and not be able to press out the foldline. Fortunately, these skinlike sewing diseases are eminently treatable. Just as we care for blisters, sunburn, poison ivy, or other superficial skin troubles with simple home remedies, here are some soothing prescriptions for superficial sewing problems.

what's inside

Ironing Accidents

Spots and Show-Through

Finicky Fibers
and Weary Weaves

66 I have a black Supplex (nylon) raincoat that I have worn forever and that I hope will never wear out. I do not know whatever possessed me, but I slapped fusible interfacing into the collar and turned-back cuffs. Of course, it bubbled. To solve the problem, I used metallic thread to stitch a diagonally quilted pattern over the collar and cuffs and picked up the metallic accent elsewhere in the garment. I have had women ask me where I found the matching texturized and quilted fabric. 99

Ironing Accidents

Let's face it, irons are dangerous contraptions. They're heavy and can break a toe or chip a ceramic tile if you drop one, and, of course, they're hot and can burn your fingers or your house down if you're not careful. Despite our healthy respect for this essential piece of sewing equipment, the iron is still the cause of many a sewing emergency. Sometimes we can blame the iron: Thermostats can fail and cause burns, soleplates get gunky with resins and starch that eventually come off on fabric, and mineral deposits clog steam vents so the iron only drips water. More often, though, ironing accidents are caused by operator error. Fortunately, there are rescues for most common ironing disasters.

Solution
When fusible interfacing bubbles

Yes, we always ought to do a test sample but sometimes we don't, and sometimes even when we carefully pre-shrink both fabric and interfacing and fuse according to directions, interfacing can bubble with subsequent cleanings as the fabrics shrink progressively.

Re-press

Particularly if you have a press or if you simply use lots of steam and elbow grease, a good press will often remove the bubbles, at least until you clean the garment again.

Pull the layers apart

Press the area to soften the fusible's resin, then carefully pull the layers of face fabric and fusible apart. Allow the area to cool and dry, and do not re-press. The interfacing will now behave like a sew-in one.

Avoiding Bubbled Interfacing

◆ *Preshrink both your garment fabric and the interfacing.*

◆ *Allow your iron to heat up thoroughly. Many models take 10 minutes or more. For most fusibles, the instructions for fusing state that your iron needs to be set to "wool" or higher so it will produce steam. If the fabric you wish to fuse must be pressed at a lower temperature, such as nylon, use a sew-in interfacing instead.*

◆ *Press the area of the garment to be interfaced, then immediately lay the interfacing in position over the fabric, and use steam only from your iron to further shrink the interfacing. You should be able to see the interfacing shrivel up as you steam it. If necessary, lift the interfacing and reposition it to keep it flat.*

◆ *Use a press cloth when you fuse. This keeps resins off your soleplate, and it slightly insulates the interfacing from the intense heat of the iron.*

◆ *Use a plain cotton ironing board cover. Avoid the metallic or Teflon kinds because these covers reflect heat back toward the interfacing, and too intense a heat may cause bubbling.*

◆ *When fusing, use an up-and-down pressing motion, not a back-and-forth ironing motion as if you were getting out wrinkles.*

◆ *Allow the fused fabrics to cool thoroughly before handling.*

◆ *If possible, launder better garments in cool water and hang to dry. Laundering in cool water and air-drying helps prevent progressive fabric shrinkage, which can cause bubbling as a garment ages since the fabric and interfacing shrink at different rates.*

Quilting or topstitching

Quilt or topstitch the area to disguise the bubbles. There are so many beautiful, decorative topstitching threads available (metallics, shiny rayons, and variegated threads) that you may end up thinking that bubbled interfacing is a blessing and an opportunity to be creative. Even if you have a simple machine, rows of utility stitches such as zigzag, blindstitch, and scallops or rows of simple embroidered motifs such as arrowheads are attractive in contrasting thread. Plain stitches can be applied in rows, like trapunto, or in grids of either squares, rectangles, or diamonds. With a darning foot, you could also stitch freehand swirls and whirls. If you have an embroidery machine, you could scatter small motifs evenly over the bubbled area.

Quilting a bubbled area distracts and decorates.

> **TIP**
>
> Beautiful topstitching threads can be tedious to sew with. Even if you use the special needles designed for this use, these threads can shred or break frequently. To avoid this problem, wind the bobbin of your machine with the decorative thread and use regular thread for the needle. Mark the interfacing side of the garment piece with your stitching design, then stitch with the interfacing up and the right side of the fabric down. Your stitching will be perfect, with no marks to remove from the right side.

Solution
For smashed pile

For washable fabrics, simply wash and machine-dry the garment to fluff up the pile. For dry-clean-only garments, use steam only from your iron or a steamer.

Steam will make the pile "bloom" before your very eyes; you can use a stiff-bristled clothes brush to help matters along.

Solution
For scorches

Let's face it: Irons can malfunction, we get distracted, and if we don't burn or melt holes in our garments, we sometimes manage to scorch them. When scorches are superficial, here is some first aid for this very painful experience.

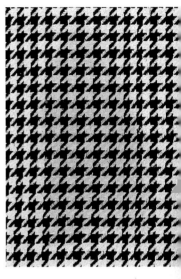

Scorches can be removed.

"*I once made a beautifully hand-tailored, three-piece suit with matching touring cap for my husband out of a worsted glen plaid. It fit him perfectly, and I had managed to match those plaids in places where no one had ever told me it was possible to match them! Anyway, I always made him model his suits for my portfolio before I allowed him to start wearing them. I decided to do a last minute, touch-up press just before this fateful little photo shoot.*

Perhaps because he was antsy while standing in my studio waiting for me, I did not allow adequate time for my iron to heat up and then cool to the proper setting, and I did not bother to use a press cloth. In the blink of an eye, there went my pride before my fall. I left a scorch the shape of the iron's soleplate smack in the middle of the lapel and collar juncture. This was like watching a child get run over by a car.

I got the scorch mark out eventually, I learned a lesson, and I earned a few more gray hairs."

Keep your iron's soleplate meticulously clean. A buildup of fibers, resins from fusible interfacings, and starch and laundry-detergent residues on your soleplate can actually cause spots on your garments. Sometimes it's all the gunk that scorches, not the fabric. Use an iron cleaner, available from sewing stores and notions catalogs, in a well-ventilated area regularly, at least once a month if you sew often. Run the iron over a terry towel, and blow vigorous steam through the vents before you press a garment since the steam vents can clog with iron cleaner, which could in itself cause spotting.

Launder or dry-clean the garment

As appropriate for the color and fiber content of the garment, use liquid chlorine bleach or dry bleach in the wash. If you take the garment to a dry cleaner, be sure to show him the scorched spot and ask him to pretreat it.

Spot-clean with detergent or spot remover

Follow the instructions on pp. 115-117 for treating oil spots. For woolens, you can also try a solution of one-half hydrogen peroxide and one-half water on the scorch as you would a spot cleaner, which will bleach woolens without yellowing. Alternate applications of detergent and water and then diluted hydrogen peroxide worked for my husband's suit.

Sand it

Use fine sandpaper. If a scorch is on a thick and fuzzy woolen, you can sometimes use fine sandpaper to lightly and carefully abrade the upper layers of scorched fibers away to reveal undamaged fabric underneath.

Solution
When press marks happen

Overly enthusiastic pressing will leave ridge lines, smashed-looking threads and fibers, and other unwanted creases and marks on garments.

Sandpaper helps remove scorched fibers.

"My 'expensive mistake' file is full of photos of $1,000 and higher suits with ridge lines along enclosed seams that were caused by inadequate grading and heavy-handed pressing. One of my favorites is a tan linen designer jacket with not only smashed-looking ridge lines all around the finished edges but also a perfectly recognizable and complete imprint of an iron's soleplate right in the middle of the lower front of the jacket. Well, at least somebody tried to press that jacket."

Use steam

Use steam only and brush the area with your fingers or a clothes brush. The steam will fluff up the area and usually eliminate the marks.

Iron imprints implicate poor pressing.

Use water in a utility sprayer

Using water in a utility sprayer, dampen the area, gently massage it with your fingers, and lightly re-press. Always test for water spotting on dry-clean-only fabrics.

Often a quick spray makes imprints go away.

❝I had to get out a bolt crease line on the purple shift with beaded mends shown in the photo on p. 14. When I bought the fabric, the friend who was shopping with me noticed that the crease was actually faded ('shopworn') on the wrong side and perhaps unremovable from the right side. She suggested that I fold the fabric when I cut it out in such a way as to avoid the crease. Of course, I completely forgot to do so. That crease down the center front of the dress would not press out, and to me, it was highly visible. Luckily, the vinegar and water solution, plus spray starch, improved matters considerably. Did you notice it?❞

Spots and Show-Through

If you are sewing and you suddenly see spots before your eyes, don't worry. It's not a vitreous hemorrhage; it's just machine oil or a pricked finger that's the cause. Likewise, when you see distracting construction details on light-colored or sheer garments, you don't need rose-colored glasses; your garment needs some simple camouflage.

Solution
For oil spills

No matter how carefully you keep your sewing area clean or how judiciously you clean and lubricate your machine, there will always be those times when an oily wad of fuzz comes unexpectedly flying out from inside the machine and lands on your garment. You can't just pretreat and launder many garments that are afflicted with the heartbreak of oil stains. Before you take the garment to the dry cleaner, here are some methods to try.

Oil spots happen.

Powdered chalk

You may have a supply of white, powdered chalk handy in your little chalk marker, the kind that uses a small, serrated wheel to leave a narrow trail of chalk on fabric to mark it. If you have a chalk-type hem marker or a refill for one, use some of that. Just sprinkle the chalk over the oil spot, allow it to sit a while, and brush away the chalk. This method seems to work best on light-colored fabrics with light-colored oil spots.

Dish detergent

Even when your fabric is dry clean only, I have had excellent results by using a dishwashing detergent that is advertised to "break up grease on contact!" This is always safe to use on polys and nylons, but even on acetate and silk duchesse satin I have not had any problems with water spotting or rings. Nevertheless, always do a test sample on a scrap.

To spot-clean, lay the oil-stained area over a clean, light-colored towel. Cover your index finger with another towel, run the tip under the faucet to moisten, and dab it on the typically soapy spout of the detergent bottle. The idea here is to use just a little water and a tiny dab of detergent. Gently scrub the stain, keeping the water and detergent mixture as isolated from the rest of the garment as possible. When the stain lifts, use a clean area of the towel, wet it, and use your fingertip to "rinse" out the detergent. Finally, blot the area between two layers of clean towel, and allow the area to dry.

> **TIP**
>
> When you clean and lube your machine (which you do regularly, right?), take care to use a brush to remove lint and fuzz from around all of the thread guides and moving parts, even if your machine is electronic and doesn't routinely require lubrication. The wads of fuzz that collect with dirt and dust plus lubricant residues are what cause black oil stains.

For small blood spots from pricked fingers, use saliva. Spit is the universal solvent. It never fails to quickly remove a blood spot. When you prick your finger, immediately moisten an uninjured fingertip and rub the spot gently until it disappears. For fabric that water spots, use the very tip of a cotton swab or a small, clean paintbrush moistened with saliva. Sewing folklore is full of assertions that bleeding on a garment is good luck for the sewer, that the garment will be successful, and that it will be well liked by its wearer. It's like a blood sacrifice!

Spot removers

There are a number of good spot removers that are available from notions catalogs, dry-cleaning-supply catalogs, and your local grocery store. Some are chalk type, some are sprayed on, and some are dabbed on. I like the kind that contains dry-cleaning fluid. You must use these with adequate ventilation, and *always* test them on a scrap.

Solution
When you have show-through

On sheer and light-colored fabrics, facings, pocket bags, most interfacings, and other construction details will show through and distract from the design of the garment. You have two options: Either surgically remove the offending detail and replace it with self-fabric or skin-toned fabric, or sometimes you can simply make another facing, pocket bag, or other detail out of skin-toned fabric, slip it under or over the original, and quickly slipstitch it in place. This "slipcover" may blend in to your liking; if not, you can always remove the slipcover, rip out the original offending detail, and then sew in the skin-colored replacement.

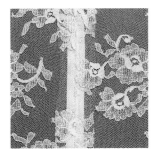

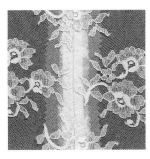

Extra layers of sheer fabrics can make a construction detail less obtrusive.

Solution
For water spots

Test this remedy on a scrap first to ensure that it does not make matters worse. Place an absorbent press cloth, such as an old gauze diaper, an artificial chamois, or a light-colored linen dishtowel, over the spot. Spray the press cloth with a fine mist from a utility sprayer and press. The extra moisture will often disburse the ring.

Solution
For pinholes

On firmly woven fabrics, ripping stitches or pinning can leave pinholes that do not easily press out. Try the following.

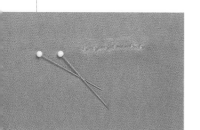

Pinholes need not be permanent.

Spit and scratch

Don't let anyone see you do this. For washable fabrics, moisten your fingertip and use your fingernail to gently rub out the holes.

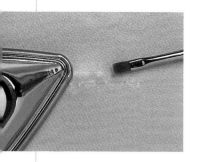

Use a fine paintbrush if your fabric water spots.

Water

Paint the holes sparingly with water using a tiny paint-brush, then cover with a press cloth and press. This will work for fabric that water spots, but of course, test on a scrap.

Finicky Fibers and Weary Weaves

Threads are the perfect size to catch on things, be it a rough fingernail, a loose prong on a ring, or your cat's claws when you want to throw it off your lap to go answer the phone. Snags and pulls are a part of life that are usually easy to deal with. Also, loosely woven fabric tends to shred, especially with wear or weight gain. There are treatments for this weakness as well.

Solution
For seam slippage

When the threads of a fabric separate into little shreds along seamlines, it's because the weave of the fabric is too loose, the fit is too tight and stresses the fabric, or the garment should have been underlined to prevent slippage. It may be after you wear a garment a few times and the fabric softens or after a weight gain that seam slippage shows up. First, do the "spit-and-scratch" maneuver. Moisten your fingertip and use your fingernail to gently realign the threads. Then use a narrow strip of fusible interfacing on the wrong side of the garment along both sides of the seamline. After fusing in place, overstitch the seam to reinforce it.

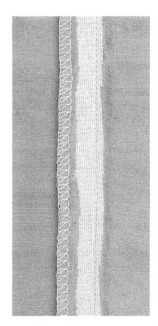

Reinforce a slipped seam with a strip of fusible interfacing.

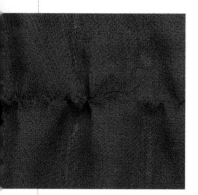

Fine fabics snag easily.

Solution
When you get pulls and snags

Pulls on woven fabrics occur when one thread gets caught on something and forms what looks like a line across the fabric. You can often stroke them out with a fingernail. Snags on knits need to be pulled inside of the garment to avoid unraveling. Do not clip them, or you may end up with holes.

The "knit picker"

A knit picker is an itty-bitty latch hook available from sewing-supply stores and notions catalogs. To use one, insert the hook from the wrong side of the garment, hook the snag, close the latch, and gently pull the snag to the wrong side of the garment. Rub the right side of the area with your fingernail to smooth.

TIP Keep an emery board close to your sewing machine to file down rough or broken nails before they snag fine fabrics.

If you don't have a knit picker, use a needle and thread.

Needle and thread

Insert the threaded, eye end of a needle from the wrong side of the garment through the base of the snag. Manipulate the snag into the loop formed by the eye end of the needle and the thread, then grasp both the needle and thread underneath, and pull the snag to the wrong side.

Solution
For letdown lines

Life will give you these, and usually they show up on your face. If you have let down a hem, however, and a visible line that will not press out remains where the hem was originally folded, you need a tonic.

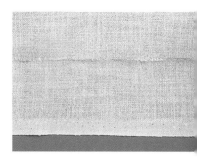

Letdown lines can be eliminated or hidden.

Vigorous brushing

Sometimes a simple brushing with a stiff-bristled clothes brush is enough to fluff up the fibers and remove lint that shows as a line. You can also try using a water and white vinegar spray as described on p. 114, and you can use spray starch to spruce up the smashed threads on the letdown line.

Laundering or dry cleaning

Launder or dry-clean the entire garment or spot-clean it. Be sure to pretreat the letdown line and press after laundering. Since letdown lines are often more of an accumulation of body oils, fuzz, and debris than just a crease, sometimes laundering alone will do the trick.

Hide it

If all else fails, cover the line with trim or decorative stitching. Try using decorative threads and embroidery stitches or rows of topstitching centered over the letdown line for a trapunto effect. Trim such as lace beading, ribbon, rickrack, or braid can resuscitate a plain, older garment and make it look contemporary and new.

Appendix A
TROUBLESHOOTING YOUR SEWING MACHINE

When you have trouble with your sewing machine or serger, you may very well feel like shooting it, but that would constitute a sewing emergency that would be beyond the scope of this book. This book can, however, help you get through most of the everyday trials and tribulations that we go through with our machines.

Have you ever noticed that even though you keep your machines cleaned, tuned, and lubed like a good little sewer that they inevitably seem to "act up" when you are tired, troubled, and running out of time? It is easy and tempting to anthropomorphically ascribe evil intent to your machines or even conversely to understand that both you and your machines need a periodic mini-vacation from sewing.

Actually, taking a break can work wonders if your machine is misbehaving. If you find yourself or your machine making too many mistakes while sewing, try getting up and taking a walk, calling a friend to chat, checking your e-mail, petting your cat, grabbing your husband and kissing him, pulling some weeds in your garden, or checking on your toddler. When I start making too many mistakes, I make myself take housework breaks, even though I hate housework, since compared with unloading the dishwasher and folding laundry, dealing with a jammed bobbin case can be a pleasure.

The reason taking a break while sewing often seems to help a persnickety machine is that most machine problems are actually caused by user error, which of course goes up when we get tired. To that effect, here are some solutions for sewing emergencies caused by the ways that we use our machines.

My thread shreds. It seems to bunch up at the eye of the needle, or sometimes it starts to shred around the tension discs.

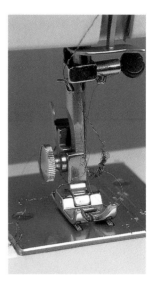

Shredding thread may have several causes.

◆ Sometimes this is caused by poor-quality thread. While all threads will have occasional weak spots, slubs, and other imperfections, cheap threads have more of them and are more likely to cause sewing problems. Do not buy the inexpensive, no-name threads in the sale basket: Invest in name-brand, high-quality machine sewing threads.

◆ Old thread naturally deteriorates, particularly if it is made of natural fibers such as cotton or silk, if made of a synthetic wrapped in a natural fiber such as cotton-wrapped polyester, or if made of decomposable synthetic fibers such as rayon. Threads older than about 10 years should be tossed. Remember, if the thread is shredding at the needle because it is old, any seams you sew with it will be weak.

◆ If the needle is too small for the diameter of thread you are using, it will be more likely to shred. Remember that you should match the size of your machine needle to the size of the thread you are using: Try a #11 with two-ply serger thread, lingerie thread, most machine-embroidery threads, and fine silk threads. Use a #14 with everyday #50 polyester, cotton-wrapped polyester, and mercerized cotton thread. Use a size 16, 18, or 20 machine needle for silk or synthetic buttonhole twist, glazed cotton, top-stitching, and other heavy, thick threads.

◆ Threads with fragile fibers such as rayon embroidery thread, metallics, and decorative plastic filament threads are naturally prone to shredding and breakage. These specialty threads require special machine needles; a large number of different types are available at your sewing store. Remember that for these decorative threads as well as for thick threads, you can always wind the difficult thread on your bobbin, use matching ordinary thread in the needle, and sew with the wrong side up.

- Rough spots on your machine's needle, throat plate, and bobbin case can shred thread. Change needles with every new project! If you find a rough spot on your throat plate, sand it off with fine sandpaper or carefully coat the area sparingly with clear nail polish and allow it to dry. If you find a rough spot on your bobbin case, take your machine in for repair.

- Try needle lubricant. Run a bodacious bead of the liquid variety along the length of the thread spool; it will soak through several layers of thread, so you will only need to reapply it periodically as you sew.

- Sew more slowly, particularly if you are using a decorative thread. Remember that the movement of thread through your machine guides and through the fabric generates considerable friction and heat; sewing slowly reduces this contributing factor.

I keep getting wads of thread on the underside of a seam as I start to sew.

These are also affectionately called "thread goobers" or alternately, "rat's nests" by us professional sewing persons. They are easily prevented:

Thread goobers are the bane of sewers.

- Always pull out 4 in. to 6 in. of thread from the needle and from the bobbin. Then make sure that the threads are underneath the presser foot and your work and that you hold both threads firmly against the machine bed with your fingers as you take the first few stitches. If the tails are too short as you start to sew, the take-up lever will pull thread backward and out of the needle (which means you have to rethread the needle, another unneeded frustration) instead of pulling thread from the spool. Your machine is not made to work that way, and the backward movement of the needle thread seems to tangle up the bobbin thread below. Note that some machines take up a very long length of thread as they start a stitch, so you would do well to get into the good habit of pulling out long tails and holding them as you sew. You wouldn't ride a horse without a firm grasp on the reins, would you? Whoa, horsie!

◆ When you remove your work from your machine, always pull it from front to back, never forward. Your machine is designed to sew best going forward, so threads are in the best working position when they are pulled to the back of the machine.

◆ Don't backstitch at the beginning of a seam. I hate it when stitches loosen up before I get a chance to sew the next cross seam to secure them, but thread goobers are far less likely if you simply shorten the stitch length for about ¼ in. to secure the threads at the start of a seam.

My machine is skipping stitches.

Run through this checklist before you take it in for repairs:

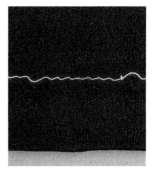

Skipped stitches cause weak seams.

◆ Change the needle. The needle may be bent or dull, or you may need to change the size or type of needle. Use a ballpoint needle on spandex or other firm knits, and use the appropriate specialty needle with specialty threads. Note that when you are sewing over elastics, machine needles of all kinds will often just "bounce" as they hit a thick strand of rubber. This will cause a skipped stitch and may even push a loop of rubber through to the wrong side of your work. If this happens, use a knit picker to pull the loop inside, and resist the urge to clip it, which might weaken the elastic.

◆ Change the tension. Loosen the upper tension slightly.

◆ Clean and lubricate the machine. Debris and friction can cause no end to performance problems.

◆ With zigzag stitches or decorative stitches, try reducing the width of the stitch slightly. If your machine's performance is a bit off, sometimes this will help.

A puckered seam is improper.

Sometimes my seams look puckered even though there are no wrinkles caught in the seam. What can I do?

Have you noticed that this happens more with some kinds of fabrics and threads than with others? There's a reason. All fabrics, on all grainlines, stretch to one degree or another. All threads stretch, too, at rates that vary with the fiber contents, the length of the fibers, the way the thread is spun, the type of stitch they are sewn into, and the length of that stitch. The trick is to try to match up all of these factors, which is not easy. In general, the more stretch in the fabric and grain, the more stretch you need in your thread and stitch. Puckering happens when the fabric stretches more than the stitches. Here are some solutions:

♦ Use a stretchier thread. Instead of 100% polyester thread, try cotton-wrapped polyester; it has a bit more stretch. Try a thinner thread such as a two-ply, since it is weaker and will stretch more than a three-ply.

♦ Stretch the fabric firmly but not forcefully in front of and behind the needle. Think of your hands as a frame, and move them forward in unison as you press the fabric against the machine bed as it feeds under the needle. This is especially important on crossgrain seams and bias seams.

♦ Let bias seams hang at least overnight before you stitch them permanently. Remember that this applies to all A-line and flared skirts, even those cut on the straight of grain. Pin-baste or very loosely hand-baste the vertical seams, then hang the garment on a hanger or dress form.

♦ Press the seam flat before you press it open. The heat from your iron shrinks the fabric against the stitches and helps discourage puckering.

♦ Underline the garment. Underlining reduces stretching.

♦ Use a stretch stitch instead of a straight stitch, or serge the seam. If your conventional machine does not sew stretch stitches specifically suitable for knits, try a narrow, fairly short zigzag stitch, and press the seam to one side.

◆ Stay the seams. Stretch the fabric gently as you sew, but stabilize the seam with a lightweight stay tape, a strip of fabric selvage, or a strip of lightweight fusible interfacing fused to one side of the seam on the wrong side.

◆ Get in the good habit of winding bobbins slowly. This reduces stretching of the bobbin thread, which reduces puckers.

◆ Sew more slowly on fabrics that tend to pucker.

◆ Reduce the needle tension slightly, but test to make sure that the machine is still forming a good-quality stitch for the sake of durability.

Sometimes my machine jams. It just won't sew at all.

◆ Have you cleaned your machine recently? Get into the good habit of cleaning it thoroughly after every project, and lubricate it after about every five projects. Even electronic machines need to be cleaned and lubricated around moving parts. Use a stiff bristled brush around all of the thread guides, the needle, and the bobbin and bobbin case. Remove the throat plate to clean underneath, and use a folded paper towel or lightweight cardboard slipped gently in between the tension discs to clean out lint and threads.

◆ Routinely rethread the machine completely, remove and replace the bobbin, and replace the needle. When you're tired and frustrated, it's easy not to notice that the machine has inadvertently come unthreaded, that you put the bobbin in its case with the thread unwinding clockwise rather than counterclockwise, or that the needle has become bent or dull.

You can't sew if your machine won't go.

◆ Remember to put the presser foot down, particularly when doing free-motion work such as darning without a presser foot in place.

◆ Use the right presser foot and corresponding throat plate for the type of stitching and the fabric you are sewing. For example, for lightweight, slippery fabrics such as silk charmeuse or chiffon, remember to change to a straight-stitch foot and throat plate. This creates more contact with fabric to the feed dogs for better control, and it prevents the needle from shoving fabric into the throat plate and jamming. For satin stitching, change to a satin stitch or embroidery foot, which has a groove underneath that allows the stitching to feed smoothly underneath the foot as you sew. Use a Teflon or roller foot on vinyl or bulky fabrics.

◆ Increase stitch length, particularly for heavy or bulky fabrics. In general, the bulkier the fabric, the longer stitches need to be to allow fabric to feed smoothly under the machine.

◆ After winding, trim the beginning end of the bobbin thread if it extends from the bobbin. It can get caught up in the leading end of the bobbin thread, needle thread, or miscellaneous moving parts.

My machine is sewing, but the stitches don't look right at all.

◆ Check the tension by switching to a straight stitch, then try the decorative stitch again.

◆ Check the stitch length and width settings recommended in your machine manual for the stitch you are trying to make. Some older, mechanical machines may also have a balance control that may need adjustment. Read your manual.

◆ Use the appropriate throat plate and foot for the stitch according to your manual.

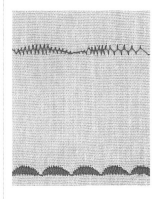

Stitch patterns can form incorrectly.

◆ Use a stabilizer on lightweight fabrics for decorative stitches.

◆ Reduce the needle tension and increase the stitch length slightly for satin stitches.

◆ For electronic machines, switch the machine off for a few minutes, then switch it on and try again. I can't explain why without babbling about Karma and the cosmos, but often this works.

◆ Keep magnets and magnetized notions such as pin holders away from your electronic machine. Magnets make very bad mojo for circuit boards.

◆ Reduce humidity and heat in your sewing area, turning on the air-conditioning if needed. Excess moisture in the air can affect your electronic machine's sensitive circuitry. This is why big computers are still housed in air-conditioned "clean rooms" to keep them happy.

◆ Keep your electronic machine on its own electrical circuit if possible. When my husband and I remodeled our garage into my studio, I had my husband wire one outlet for my electronic machine only, so it was the only appliance on that circuit and had its own breaker. This has improved its behavior considerably. Before, I used an "outlet stick" for my machine and half a dozen other electric appliances. Whenever I turned on my radio, my machine acted up, and it wasn't because it didn't like classical music. My husband the electrical engineer assured me that yes, other appliances on the same circuit can and do cause interference with sensitive circuit boards.

◆ Check the switch for twin needles. Make sure it is set appropriately. On my electronic machine, the switch sometimes jiggles itself down, or maybe I or a cat bump it. If it is set for twin needles and you are using a single needle, the result can be buttonholes and other stitches sewn at about half their normal width; if vice versa, the result will be broken needles or worse.

There's a reason your needle keeps breaking.

I keep breaking needles. It drives me crazy.

◆ Don't sew over pins unless you absolutely have to. For matching plaids and intersecting seams, I sew over pins slowly while advancing the needle with the handwheel only, so the needle slides past the pin instead of hitting it with enough force to break, bend, or blunt the needle.

◆ Don't sew over metal zipper teeth or stops.

◆ Don't sew over beads or sequins. To sew seams on beaded or sequined fabrics, carefully fit the garment, then remove beads and sequins from the seam allowances by carefully pulling them from the cut threads along the cut edges of each garment piece. Put the beads or sequins aside.

Secure the loose threads to the seam allowances with fabric glue and allow the glue to dry thoroughly, or fuse narrow strips of fusible interfacing along the cut edges on the right side of the seam allowances. Then sew the seam using a zipper foot, keeping the foot snug up against the beads or sequins.

Open the seam with steam and your fingers only (do not iron open the seam), and apply the saved beads or sequins along the right side of the seamline by hand or with fabric glue to fill in any bald or sparse areas.

◆ Make sure you are using the right presser foot and throat plate. For zigzag stitches, for example, you must switch from a straight-stitch foot and throat plate to the zigzag ones. Likewise, when straight stitching, you must use the zigzag throat plate and foot if you shift the needle position to the right or left from the center position.

◆ Use the right size and type of needle for your machine and for your fabric, and insert it properly. If you use a #11 needle in six layers of heavy denim or if you manage to stick a needle in its clamp backward, I can guarantee it will break.

◆ Check if the needle is hitting any part of the machine. Particularly if you hear clinking noises, stop immediately! Check if the needle is bent; check if the presser foot has snapped off or is not screwed on tightly; check if any loose pins or pieces of broken needle have fallen into the bobbin mechanism; and check if the bobbin case is seated properly. If these things pass inspection, then open up the throat plate, very slowly advance the handwheel, and look carefully to see and hear if and where the needle is hitting metal. If you still hear a clink or if you see the needle hitting anything, take your machine in for repair before you do any more damage.

◆ Keep lots of extra needles on hand. Let's face it, they break easily, and it's better to replace a bent or dull one or simply replace it routinely with each garment than risk damaging an expensive sewing machine.

My serger sometimes pulls fabric into a fold as it passes the cutting blades, which wads it up around the foot, messes up the stitches, and doesn't trim the seam allowance off neatly.

Sometimes sergers do not handle lofty fabrics well.

◆ Change the lower cutting blade. Keep an extra one on hand because they do get dull and how often you will need to replace one depends on how much you serge and what types of materials you have been working on. Metallics such as lamés, silks, and polyesters will dull the blades more quickly than cottons and woolens. Note that the upper blade will seldom if ever need changing, unless of course you serge over a pin, which is an expensive mistake that you will probably only make once. Do not even think about running beaded or sequined fabrics through your serger's knives without removing the crunchy bits first, as described on the facing page.

◆ Examine the lower cutting blade for nicks and other damage, and replace if needed. Also, check that the top of the blade is perfectly even with the top of the throat plate. Sometimes the blade will vibrate loose and slip down slightly so it is not aligned properly with the upper blade and does not cut well, just as a pair of scissors with a loose screw or bent blades will not cut well. Loosen the setscrew that holds the lower blade in place very slightly, and move the blade up. Feel with the fingernail of your left hand that the blade and the throat plate are level and even, then tighten the setscrew.

◆ Hold the fabric slightly firmly in front of and behind the needle, and guide it into the knives flat and level to the throat plate. This works for the same reason that cutting fabric with shears at right angles to the fabric works better than holding the shears at an acute or oblique angle.

◆ For thick or lofty fabrics, compress the material with your fingers as it goes under the blades. Serge slowly. To serge over bulky seam allowances, try advancing the needle with the handwheel, and visually check that the upper knife clears and then cuts the loft of the fabric with each stitch.

My serger will not form stitches properly.

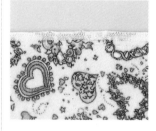

Analyze improperly formed serger stitches with calm observation.

◆ Check that the serger is threaded properly, following your manual very carefully. You must not miss one thread guide; you must thread the right needles in the right needle positions; you must thread them in the correct sequence for the stitch you want to produce; and you must have the tensions adjusted appropriately for the stitch you desire. Stay calm, and take a break if you get too frustrated. Some sergers that make numerous types of stitches are very complicated indeed, and it takes time and patience to learn to thread them.

◆ Check your serger for all problems that cause incorrectly formed stitches in conventional machines: bent or wrong needles, wrong presser foot or plate, dirty or in need of lubrication, poor-quality thread.

My serger is sewing puckered seams.

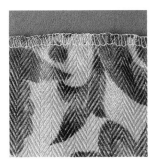

◆ On a conventional serger, try stretching the fabric slightly in front of and behind the needle as you serge; changing the stitch length or type of stitch; stabilizing the seam with fusible interfacing or stay tape; or changing the weight of the thread.

◆ If your machine has differential feed, simply adjust it until the puckers are eliminated.

Puckered serger seams are easy to eliminate.

Sometimes when I serge knits they get all stretched out and lose their shape.

◆ Stabilize the seam with strips of fusible interfacing or stay tape. Clear elastic makes a wonderful stabilizer for necklines and shoulder seams, since nicks from serger blades will not damage it and it is not bulky.

◆ Do not pull the fabric in front of the needle. Allow it to feed naturally. Support the fabric with your hands as it moves under the needle instead of allowing it to pull down off the table or off of your lap.

◆ Staystitch seams or baste them with your conventional machine to avoid excessive stretching during normal handling and fitting.

◆ For prepleated fabrics, stabilize the pleats with strips of package wrapping tape along each seam and hemline, just to one side so the tape is not inside the seam or hem allowances. Do not serge or sew over adhesive tape, or the needle may draw adhesive onto moving machine parts.

◆ Don't remove pattern tissues from the cut garment pieces until you are just ready to sew them. The pattern tissue will temporarily help stabilize the pieces.

◆ Switch from a very stretchy three-thread to a less stretchy four-thread or five-thread safety stitch. This is especially useful for moderately stretchy double knits and for ribbing.

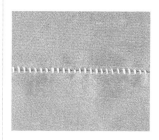

Railroaded seams are weak and unattractive.

From the right side of the garment, I can see the stitches in the seam.

◆ Increase the needle tension and/or loosen the lower looper tension. The seam is flat-locking and would pull open completely with wear.

◆ Shorten the stitch length. More stitches will relieve stress on the seam, which will help reduce flat-locking.

◆ Switch to a four-thread or five-thread safety stitch.

◆ Topstitch the seam from the garment right side on your conventional machine with a zigzag or multiple zigzag stitch. This is a very durable but very stretchy treatment for shapewear and activewear.

EMERGENCY SUPPLIES: THE FIRST-AID KIT FOR SEWERS

If you have the following sewing supplies, tools, and techniques at hand, you will be ready for action when your next sewing emergency strikes. Nearly all of these items are readily available at your local sewing store or through notions catalogs.

Supplies

Alcohol No, not the 80-proof variety, even though it might calm you down after you have slashed through the front of your daughter's wedding gown, but ordinary rubbing alcohol from the family medicine chest. Use it to remove residue from fusible webs that have strayed onto visible garment areas. Foil-wrapped alcohol swabs are handy to keep in your sewing area for this purpose.

Backer buttons Backer buttons are perfectly plain, typically clear plastic buttons. Use them as a substitute for more expensive buttons where they will not show. Backer buttons also help strengthen and stabilize large buttons that take a great deal of stress on thick or easily torn materials, such as for heavy coats, leather garments, or on garments made of loosely woven, lofty fabrics such as mohair coatings or tweeds.

For reinforcement, select backer buttons with the same number of holes as the buttons on the right side of the garment. The backer buttons can be smaller than the outside buttons. First, position the backer button on the wrong side of the overlap at the button placement mark. Secure the thread at the mark on the right side of the garment, and bring it up through the underside of the outside button. Then insert the needle down through the hole opposite, through the garment, and through the corresponding hole of the backer button, as if making a button, garment, button sandwich. Next, insert the needle through the opposite hole on the backer button, the garment, and the outside button.

Remember to form a thread shank the thickness of the garment as you sew between the outside button and the garment, while keeping the backer button flat to the wrong side. You do this by holding the outside button slightly away from the garment with your nimble fingers as you sew. Finally, wrap the thread around the shank a few times, and take three or four tiny stitches on top of one another at the base of the shank on the garment right side to secure the thread. Insert the needle into the garment at the base of the shank, then bring it out through the layers of fabric to the facing seam and cut the thread close.

Do you remember the old admonition, "A stitch in time saves nine"? When you sew a button on right in the first place, like this, it will stay on for the life of the garment.

Beeswax Often the simplest, most basic sewing supplies are the ones that are the best and most useful. Purchase a piece of beeswax from your notions supplier or, in a pinch, buy a beeswax candle. If you are truly desperate, use paraffin from a grocery store (check with the canning supplies) or from a white candle. You should run all hand-sewing threads over beeswax several times before sewing. Beeswax performs the following beatific miracles.

◆ It lubricates the thread and helps prevent tangling as you sew, which can otherwise drive you mad. Since most modern sewing-machine threads are designed to work with stretchy fabrics, they stretch too, and that contributes to tangling. Also, polyester threads pick up static as you pull the thread through fabric, and the static causes tangling. This is also why sewing s-l-o-w-l-y will help if your thread is tangling and why silk thread and glazed cotton thread tangle less and are better suited for hand sewing than machine threads. Wax them, too!

◆ It strengthens threads. The beeswax coats the threads, which helps prevent abrasion as the threads move against the garment during normal wear and cleanings. I have cut the buttons off of 20-year-old jackets that were going to their great reward, and even through decades of wear and dry cleaning, I could still feel the wax in the button shanks.

◆ It "glues" multiple strands of threads together so they act as one. If you like to save time by sewing on buttons with four or even eight strands of thread at a time, wax the thread strand singly as you thread the needle, then wax the multiple strands together as you begin to sew. Re-wax the multiple strands after you sew each button to straighten the threads, align, and lubricate them.

Although some sewers recommend running a waxed thread over your hot iron before you begin to sew to "melt the wax into the thread," I think that this exercise merely results in waxing your ironing-board cover. Since the act of pulling a thread through fabric produces friction and, locally, great heat, just taking one or two stitches produces the same effect. If a couple of tiny flakes of excess wax are deposited at the base of the stitch as you begin to sew, simply flick them away with your fingernail. In my 30-some years of hand sewing, I have never found that beeswax caused any mark or stain on any fabric.

Bleach Using *chlorine bleach* and hot water in your washing machine removes oil stains and some scorches, but do not use bleach on woolens, nylons, spandex or Lycra, and acetates because it will weaken and discolor these fibers.

Hydrogen peroxide is an alternative bleach that is readily available wherever first-aid supplies are sold. Dilute it by half with water to safely bleach washable wools, but always test first.

Boning (plastic or spiral steel) Plastic boning, also called feather boning (comes from plastic chickens), is available in packages or by the yard. It is inexpensive, easy to find, and can be cut and shaped with scissors. It is used to provide support

and shape to garments, particularly to strapless dresses and to raised waistbands and collars. It can also remove unwanted curls from collars and lapels.

Spiral-steel boning is a bit harder to find. It comes precut in a range of lengths, or you can buy a roll of it (it looks like something you could use for a plumbing emergency). To use it, you need to cut it to length using pliers and strong hands, and then use household glue and pliers to put metal tips on the ends. Spiral steel is very much worth the trouble. It flexes in all directions, it's thin, and it doesn't rust—it was formerly used in swimsuits. It is available from Greenberg and Hammer, 24 W. 57th St., New York, NY 10019-3918, (800) 955-5135.

Collar stays Collar stays are short pieces of narrow plastic about 2 in. long that are designed to slip into little rectangular pockets on the underside of the collars of men's dress shirts. They have one squared and one pointed end, which fits the point of the collar. They prevent the corner of collars from curling up and help them form a sharp-looking convex bow against the upper chest area. For the same reason, they are useful in women's collars and can be added to straighten curly collars after construction is completed. It's best to remove them before laundering or they will as often as not end up in the lint trap of your dryer.

Elastic braid Elastic braid is more rigid and keeps its stretch longer than knitted elastic. Good widths to keep on hand are ¼ in., ⅜ in., ⅝ in., and ⅞ in. If you come upon skin-toned elastic, put some away for your next sheer project.

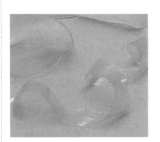

Elastic (clear) Clear elastic comes in various widths; ⅜ in. and ⅝ in. are handy. You'll find it with other packaged elastics. Clear elastic is extremely stretchy and flexible but very thin, and it is soft and comfortable against the skin, which makes it especially suitable for use in lingerie and swimwear. It is also well suited for serger application, since nicking it with serger knives will not affect its durability or stretch.

Elastic thread Elastic thread comes cross-wound on a spool in black and white, although sometimes you will come upon decorative colors as well. The rubber in this elastic will deteriorate over many years, so don't bother using that 10-year-old spool in your sewing drawer. This thread is handy for easing out excess width around necklines, for elasticizing garment openings on babies' and children's clothes, and for easy smocking effects.

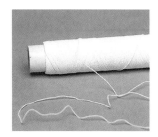

Hook-and-loop tape Hook-and-loop tape can be purchased by the yard or in packages, in strips, dots, or squares, in different degrees of flexibility and strength, and in various colors. I like the cheap, white kind that comes in bundles. Remember that you can cut these strips up into very small pieces, such as a ¼-in. square, and use them as substitutes for snaps or buttons.

Fusible basting thread This is a thread version of bonding web. It looks like a thick thread and is best used in the bobbin of your machine. Because of its thickness, you may need to bypass your bobbin case's tension guides. I find that this thread version of fusible material does not quite "stick" as well as the strip or paper-backed types. Use it to temporarily hold garment pieces in place before you secure them conventionally with stitching.

Fusible interfacing Available in a range of colors, fiber contents, widths, textures, opacity, and crispness, fusible interfacing is very helpful to have on hand. Do not purchase the kind for crafts that is sold precut in plastic bags. Brand-name interfacings sold on bolts are better quality.

Fusible web This is the "glue" that sticks fusible interfacing to fabric, although you can use it to fuse any heat-tolerant fabric to another. Paper-backed fusible agent is sold on bolts with the interfacings. Since these fusible webs add various degrees of stiffness to any area to which they are applied, choose accordingly. Some are marketed to be softer than others, and some are quite stiff and are most suitable for crafts.

Strips of fusible webbing are also sold on rolls; the ¼-in. and ⅝-in. widths are good to have on hand. Serge fusible web strips to the wrong side of straight hems to finish the raw edge, then turn up the hem and simply press it in place to secure. Try this on satins and other shiny fabrics that show the tiniest of hand hem stitches. To keep facings from rolling to the outside of garments, slip ¼-in. to 1-in. pieces of webbing between the shoulder seams and facing seams at necklines and fuse in place. Slip pieces of webbing underneath the outside edges of the wrong side of patch pockets, fuse, then topstitch without slipping and without pins.

Iron cleaner Iron cleaner comes in a tube and is available wherever notions are sold. Irons naturally accumulate all sorts of gunk on their soleplates: starch deposits, resins from fusibles, and microscopic fiber bits. In the old days, we used to run our irons over waxed paper to make them glide over laundry better, which in effect waxed the gunk, not the soleplates. Iron cleaners actually remove the gunk.

Remember to run your cleaned iron over a towel and blast steam enthusiastically through the steam vents to clean the cleaner out of the holes because these petroleum-based products can themselves leave greasy marks on clothes if you do not remove them thoroughly from your iron. Keep the cleaners off of your ironing-board cover for the same reason.

Needle lubricant Needle lubricant is a silicone-based product that does for machine threads what beeswax does for hand-sewing threads. Particularly on microfibers, vinyls, and hi-tech nylon fabrics that are windproof and water resistant, such as Supplex and Taslan, the mechanical action of thread and needle moving at high speeds through closely spaced threads and fibers produces so much friction and heat that polyester threads can actually melt as you sew.

I finally figured this out the hard way while making buttonholes on a Supplex raincoat. I was using a Microtex needle, but the thread kept breaking over and over again. Finally, after close inspection, I saw that the thread looked like shiny plastic where it had broken, and I realized that it had actually melted.

By using a needle lube and sewing very slowly, I was finally able to complete the buttonholes.

Liquid needle lube that comes in a bottle can be applied by running a bountiful bead down the length of your thread spool, where a bit will be soaked in to every 1 in. or so of thread. Reapply the bead to the spool periodically as you sew. Thicker needle lube that comes in a tube is meant to be dotted onto a little sponge applicator housed in a little container that is affixed to your machine head or to a thread holder strand, where your needle thread is passed over the sponge so the lube is applied as you sew.

Check your machine's manual to determine whether your tension discs are made of rubber, which should not be exposed to silicone products because they may deteriorate them. Also, while needle lubes are not supposed to cause stains, I would keep them away from grease magnets like white silk-satin wedding gowns!

Safety pins Don't laugh. We all need them, even if we sew. Small ones are best; try to find some that are not flimsy so they do not pop open and really injure you. Keep a few in your handbag for garment emergencies.

You can also use safety pins as lingerie guards. Simply pin them into a shoulder seam allowance, parallel to the seamline, with the head side of the pin toward the shoulder seam. Carefully slip the pin end under your strap and close the pin.

Sandpaper (fine) Just a small piece of fine sandpaper is all I hope you will ever need. Use it to remove pills from fuzzy fabrics as well as to remove scorch marks.

Seam rippers Of course you must have these for everyday sewing 911's, yet there are various types available, and some are more suited for certain disasters than others.

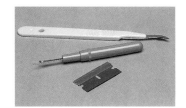

The very tiny conventional rippers that are about 3 in. long have small points and will save you time and grief when ripping out very short stitches. The small handles can get tiresome to hold onto, especially for stiff or arthritic hands or for sewers with large fingers.

The larger seam rippers that are about the size of a ballpoint pen are more comfortable to hold and use for long periods of time, but the points are fatter and harder to slip under closely spaced stitches.

To rip stitches using either size conventional ripper, you slip the pointed end under the stitch, push the tool forward so the stitch slides into the sharp curve of the C-shaped end, and slice the stitch. For ripping out seams, you can rip every third or fourth stitch from one side of the seam, then pull the thread on the opposite side up in one continuous piece. Brush away the clipped threads on the other side with your hands or clothes brush. Note that this method avoids marring the fabric.

For sturdy fabrics, it is faster to pull the layers of the seam open with one hand, insert the ripper into the stitches, rip out a stitch, pull the seam open about ½ in., rip another stitch, and repeat until the seam is opened. Take care not to pull too hard on the seam allowances; the goal is to expose the next intact stitch but not to rip or mar the fabric itself.

One type of seam ripper that is actually a surgical tool consists of a metal handle, sometimes mounted in a larger plastic handle, with a scalpel-sharp, hook-shaped blade on the end. To use it, you slip the hooked end under a stitch and cut it. This tool is particularly useful when ripping serged seams, since you can slip several loops under the tool and sever them with one stroke. The blade on this ripper is dangerously sharp, so use it with care, and be sure to put it away in its plastic sheath when not in use.

Single-edged razor blades are a threat to fabrics and fingers, but many experienced sewers swear by them for ripping. Do you like to live dangerously? Use the blade by holding it by the dull edge and pulling the fabric layers apart with one hand as you slice stitches with the sharp edge. Take care to cover the sharp edge of the blade after you use it, and hide it from children of all ages.

Seam sealant Do you remember using blobs of clear nail polish to stop runs on pantyhose? Seam sealant is a liquid product along those lines, only it's made to stop fraying. It is not water soluble, so laundering does not remove it. Use seam sealant to give body and prevent raveling on machine button-holes, to prevent ravels and add strength to clipped seams, to prevent serged seams from coming undone, and to dot onto very small holes and snags in garments to prevent them from becoming larger. There are various small nozzles from your notions supplier that can allow you to place very small dots of sealant exactly where you want it, rather than the large blob that typically gushes out of the bottle. You can also use a fine paintbrush for accurate application.

Be aware that on rare occasions, seam sealant may not dry invisibly and may leave a dark stain. Fortunately, this stain can often be removed. It is always wise to test on a scrap, particularly on microfiber fabrics (see "Alcohol" on p. 135).

Skin-toned fabric When you manage to find a lightweight, firmly woven cotton that looks like you, grab a couple of yards and salt it away for your next sheer project. Use it for pocket bags, facings, casings, and other inside garment components where it may be less obtrusive than self-fabric.

Snaps Snaps are useful in a variety of sizes and colors, from itty-bitty to very large. You will find them in silver, black, and clear plastic. The clear ones blend in so well that you may have to put your glasses on to get dressed. Sometimes the plastic ones are defective, so check that they actually snap together before you sew them on.

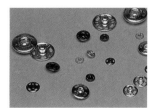

Spot cleaners Spot cleaners include white chalk, grease-cutting dish detergent, and dry-cleaning solvents. The solvent-type spot removers are available at grocery stores in the laundry supplies aisle. Try these on your dry-clean-only projects before you give up and take them to the dry cleaner. You should also keep laundry-type spot removers on hand. I find that the stick kinds work better on grease spots than the spray varieties.

Stay tapes Stay tapes are handy to have in various forms. Twill tape is a sturdy woven tape that comes in ¼-in. and ½-in. widths, in black and white, and on rolls or in packages; it is often sold from the display of rickrack and bias bindings. Try to find twill tape that is made of cotton rather than polyester, since you can use its shrinkable nature to help you remove excess ease where you don't want it, such as on the roll line of a lapel. Stay Tape is a brand of translucent tricot tape. Strips of lightweight selvage, such as that of silk organza, are also useful.

All stay tapes are used to stabilize areas that might stretch excessively with wear, such as along the side seamline of pants where you would attach pocket bags. They also hold and stabilize areas from which you have removed extra ease that you do not want, such as on gaping necklines, roll lines, and areas of stress. To apply stay tapes by machine, simply center them over the area you wish to stay, and machine-stitch them to the garment just inside the seamline or roll line. By hand, for finer garments, use a fell stitch along each side of the tape to invisibly attach it to the face fabric, underlining, or interfacing.

Tweezers Tweezers with flat rather than pointed tips are valuable for pulling out ripped stitches, threads, and errant fibers that have become caught in seams and topstitching. Don't bother with your old eyebrow-plucking tweezers that are no longer properly aligned and couldn't grab a splinter if you tried. Shell out $10 for a pair that really works. If your hands are arthritic or your nails are short, tweezers can save pain and time when ripping.

Vinegar (white) White vinegar can both set and help remove creases. Dilute it with water by 50%, and keep it handy in a utility sprayer for easy application.

Equipment

Clothes brush Every closet and every sewing room should have a clothes brush. This is a large, stiff-bristled brush that will help you restore crushed nap and remove wrinkles, fuzz, threads, hair, dust, and you don't want to think of what else from your clothes between cleanings. They are available from The Fuller Brush Co., One Fuller Way, Great Bend, KS 67530, (316) 792-1711, www.fuller.com.

Ham (pressing) This firmly stuffed pressing aid is shaped vaguely like a ham, the type that comes in cans that you keep on the pantry shelf in case of hurricanes or emergency social events. The curves of a pressing ham reproduce the various curves of the human body, so pressing relatively flat fabric over a ham allows that fabric to take the shape of those curves.

A pressing ham is essential for the construction of tailored garments, but try using it also for everyday ironing when you press around darts, curved garment pieces such as cuffs and collars, and other areas that cover our curves. Your clothes will suddenly look more expensive, as if they were made for you. Pressing hams are available wherever sewing supplies are sold. Every sewer should have one.

Hem markers Not all of us have a patient sewing friend or trainable spouse to help us pin up hems easily and evenly. Fortunately, we can buy or create helpers.

Here's an old-fashioned method: Take a piece of kitchen string and run it over a piece of chalk several times. Thumbtack the string at your desired hem height across the frame of an open doorway, making sure the string is level by measuring the frame up from the floor evenly on each side. Put on the dress or skirt, and gently twirl up against the string so the chalk leaves a mark on the garment.

You can purchase hem markers at sewing-supply stores and through notions catalogs. The pin-type requires a helper; the chalk type squirts a line of chalk on the garment with the squeeze of a bulb.

Knit picker Look among the notions for this tiny latch hook that will rescue snags. For instructions on how to use it, see p. 120.

Permanent markers, acrylic paints, nail polish

Rummage through your office supplies, craft supplies, and cosmetics case to cure the following sick situations.

If you find that light-colored interfacing shows through cut buttonholes on dark-colored garments (yes, you should have used black or gray interfacing, but most of us don't keep it around), just run the tip of a matching permanent felt marker around the cut edge of the buttonhole. Colors need to blend but do not always need to match. Test on a small area only, step back, and judge whether this helps or hinders. This nearly always works well for black fabrics.

If you are making covered buttons and your fabric is loosely woven, the shine of the metal button form often shows through. Using two layers of fabric or adding a thin lining works only if the fabrics are very thin. For bulky fabrics, use permanent marker, nail polish, acrylic paints, or even typewriter correction fluid to "prime" the metal button forms. Be sure to allow them to dry thoroughly before covering the buttons. Again, colors for the primer coat may not need to match but may only need to blend.

Press cloth

A piece of washed muslin with the edges pinked or serged, an old gauze diaper, or a white linen tea towel will do nicely as a press cloth.

Sleeve roll

This is a firm, cylindrical-shaped pressing aid that is available from sewing stores and notions catalogs. Use it to press open seams inside hard-to-reach areas such as sleeves and collars. Also, use a sleeve roll for pressing open seams on fragile fabrics that leave press marks, such as on taffeta and satins.

Steamer

Most household irons are not designed primarily to produce steam, even though steam will get you out of more sewing disasters than heat. Use steam to help garments drape gracefully, to set soft pleats in skirts and draperies, and to revive crushed pile.

There are small, hand-held steamers that double as travel irons that work well. I always recommend to brides that someone in the bridal party bring one along and that her attendants allow time to steam out wrinkles in one another's gowns between dressing and the ceremony, before all photos, and between the ceremony and the reception. Weddings usually require a certain amount of driving around in formal attire, which involves sitting and which almost always creates wrinkles.

Look for a steamer that uses tap water; some older ones only work if you add salt to the water. A larger, floor-model steamer produces clouds of blasting steam in minutes and is a worthwhile investment for serious sewers. It can also cut down dramatically on the time it takes to remove wrinkles from the family laundry.

If you don't have a steamer, remember the bathroom trick. Put the wrinkled garment on a hanger or hang yardage from the shower-curtain rod. Put the plug in the tub, turn on the hot water full blast, and close the bathroom door. Remember to turn off the water when the tub is full! Keep the door closed for about 30 minutes or until the steam dissipates. A customer once brought me a piece of rayon velvet for a skirt that had been crushed and wadded up in a plastic bag in the bottom of her closet for at least 10 years. It was a mess, but after 30 minutes of steam in my bathroom, the velvet looked perfect.

Steam iron You must have an iron that produces copious quantities of steam. Even if your iron's instructions state that you do not need to use distilled water, eventually you will get a buildup of minerals from tap water in the holes in the sole-plate, which may make your iron drip or even prevent it from steaming altogether.

Utility sprayer You can find utility sprayers at grocery or kitchen-gadget stores. Use them with water to press creases either in or out, or fill them with a 50% water and white vinegar solution to more permanently set creases or to remove them.

> **TIP**
>
> To clean out the mineral buildup from your iron, try this: Fill the water chamber with white vinegar, heat the iron to "cotton," iron a towel, then allow the iron to sit for about an hour. Empty out the vinegar, rinse out the chamber a few times, and refill it with water. Iron some more to work water vapor through the steam vents. The vinegar should remove the mineral deposits so the iron will produce more steam.

Appendix C
STAIN REMOVAL

For all of us who wear clothes and particularly for those of us who invest in the time, expertise, and expense that it takes to sew our own clothes, stains on garments constitute a disaster that can often be successfully treated at home. In fact, many of us who sew delight in being able to launder garments that if purchased as ready-to-wear would otherwise need dry cleaning, since we can preshrink our fabrics and trims while clothing manufacturers would not bother to do so. So sewers are more likely to launder than to run to the dry cleaner. It's helpful, therefore, to have a supply of materials and techniques on hand for stain removal for those days when the normal spills and slops of outrageous fortune are the disaster du jour.

Know your fiber content

The chemical compositions of fabrics vary with their fiber contents and so must the chemicals used to treat stains on fabrics vary accordingly. Fiber is the actual material from which threads are spun and then woven or knitted into fabrics. As a home sewer, you may need to make a special effort to deduce the fiber content of your fabrics, particularly if you purchase "mystery fabrics." By federal law, all textiles must be labeled with fiber content by percentages and country of origin; in practice, many textiles are mislabeled or simply not identified at all.

As an aid to memory, you may wish to keep a notebook of the fiber contents of your fabric purchases for future reference. Was that an all-flax, all-cotton, or poly-blend white, four-year-old shirt that you slopped red wine on? Do you dare use chlorine bleach on it? That depends on fiber content. If you didn't keep a note on fiber content, you can burn-test a scrap of fabric, a tiny snip from a hem or seam allowance, or even a few pulled threads from an unfinished edge inside the garment (see the chart on p. 152 for basic burn-testing guidelines).

Here are some specific tips about particular types of fibers. Note that for blends, a combination of fiber characteristics will affect stains.

Natural fibers Cotton, rayon, ramie, lyocel, linen (made from flax fiber), Tencel, and other cellulosic fibers are weakened by repeated use of liquid chlorine bleach, but it can be used occasionally for stain removal. Protein fibers such as silk, wool, and luxury woolens such as cashmere and camel hair are damaged by even a weak dilution of chlorine bleach, which will also cause yellowing. Stiffening, weakening, and color loss can also occur.

Synthetics Acetate, triacetate, and modacrylic fibers can dissolve in acetone (fingernail-polish remover) or paint thinner. Acrylic, nylon, polyester, and olefin attract oils, both from foods and from body oils. Oil stains must be treated quickly for removal, or they may be permanent. Heat from your dryer can set oil stains permanently, so air-dry a garment that you have treated for an oil stain and check for success before machine-drying. Vinyl and natural rubber materials can be damaged by oil-based solvents, which include petroleum-based prewash sprays. Olefins can be damaged by some dry-cleaning solvents and not by others.

Basic stain-removal supplies

◆ **White terry towels and paper towels.** Do not use printed paper towels or colored towels. Dyes can bleed onto the fabric you are treating and could make matters worse!

◆ **Bleaches.** Liquid chlorine bleach must be diluted with water or it can weaken and yellow many fibers and can actually dissolve and form holes in wools and silks. All-fabric bleach, which comes in dry or liquid form, is safer but less powerful. Hydrogen peroxide is so gentle it is used to bleach human hair; it is safe to use with protein fibers in diluted form.

◆ **Detergents.** Read labels carefully. Some detergents are light duty, meant for hand-washing delicate garments in

TIP

There are some fabrics that can neither be dry-cleaned nor laundered. I have seen samples of a crystal-pleated, metallic-silk-blend organza, for example, and glued-on sequined fabrics that were labeled "Do not wash; do not dry-clean." Go figure.

cool water; they are not meant for greasy coveralls or grass-stained children's clothes. If you pay extra for detergents with bleaches or fabric softeners, note that they may not be as effective as using a regular detergent plus separate additives. The term "heavy duty" describes detergents with the greatest capacity for stain removal.

◆ **Pretreatment products**. Petroleum-based solvents (read those labels) come in spray, stick, and gel forms. These are especially useful on oil-based stains.

◆ **Not so basic but often necessary.** Also good to have on hand are rubbing alcohol (for felt markers, some pen inks); ammonia (handy for skunk); color remover such as Rit; dry-cleaning fluid-based spot remover; rust-remover products such as Whink or Rit; turpentine (for fresh, oil-based paint); white vinegar (for removing urine odors and stains); lemon juice and salt (sometimes works on rust); and nail-polish remover (for nail polish on fabrics other than acetate, modacrylic, and triacetate).

Determine the type of stain If you weren't present mentally and physically when the stain occurred, you can sometimes deduce its origin by its location on the garment. For example, we usually slop foods down the fronts of garments; grease stains often show up on pants and skirts where they rub on car-door hinges and latches; and perspiration occurs naturally around the neckline, under the arms, and under the bust on tight-fitting garments. Colors can give you clues, but they may be misleading. A caramel-colored stain, for example, might be from coffee, the sugar in white wine or clear soda, rust, makeup, or any manner of materials. Try the following treatments for the following groups of stains.

◆ **Oil-based stains.** These include mayonnaise, gasoline, cooking fats and oils, body oils, and oily cosmetics. Use a petroleum-based pretreatment product as soon as possible. The sticks work better than the liquids. If you don't have a petroleum-based pretreatment product, rub on undiluted liquid heavy-duty detergent or a paste of powdered heavy-duty detergent mixed with hot water.

> **TIP**
>
> Remember never to mix stain-removal chemicals; some combinations, such as bleach and ammonia, produce toxic fumes. This particular gas was called mustard gas during World War I and killed thousands of people. Follow all cautions on product labels: Store products carefully and out of the reach of children; avoid skin contact; avoid inhaling products and ensure adequate ventilation; and do not use products near an open flame or an electrical outlet.

Then launder in the hottest water that is safe for the fiber content of the garment. Inspect before machine-drying; repeat if needed.

◆ **Protein stains.** These include blood, egg yolk and white, milk (and milk products such as pudding, baby formula, and cheese), vomit, urine, feces, white glue or paste, mucus, and Jello. These are the stains of life, are they not? First, soak these stains in cold water and agitate them (hot water cooks and sets the stains). Then launder with detergent in warm but not hot water. You may need to repeat using an appropriate bleach for brightly colored stains.

◆ **Stains from dyes.** Causes may include paints, mustard, color bleeding, inks, some fruit stains such as cherry and blueberry, artificial food colors, and grass stains. Start by pretreating the stain with heavy-duty detergent, then rinse. Next, soak it in water with all-fabric bleach. If that does not work, try chlorine bleach for appropriate fibers in water for 15 minutes; longer than that only weakens fibers. Note that rubbing alcohol can remove some pen inks if used quickly: Simply pour it over the spot and rinse the garment before laundering.

◆ **Stains from tannins.** Tannins are astringent chemicals from plants that often turn things brown, hence the word "tan." They come from beverages such as tea, beer, coffee, tomato juice, fruit juice, soft drinks, wine, and hard liquors and from some perfumes. Typically, normal laundering will remove them, but they may need bleaching, especially if they are old stains. Do not use bar soap or natural soap, such as that designed for baby clothes, since they are likely to set stains from tannins.

◆ **Combinations of stains.** So it was a really wild party. Not really; many stains come from products that are a combination of ingredients. Most are a combination of oil-based plus dye-based stains, so treat for both: Use a dry-cleaning solvent or petroleum-based pretreatment for oily materials first, then rub detergent into the area and launder with a fiber-appropriate bleach.

Appendix D
BURN TESTING FOR FIBER CONTENT

You don't need to be a chemist in a laboratory to determine the fiber content of "mystery fabrics." The following tests give good indications but not scientific proof, and blends can be particularly tricky to determine. Nevertheless, these tests, along with your hands and your experience with the feel of various fabrics, are much better than nothing as you start to sew, press, and treat stains in a fabric.

You may wish to make a little kit to keep in your handbag and take with you to fabric stores for burn testing. Most stores will give you a little snip of fabric, although you should always conduct the test outdoors so you do not burn the store down and generally disrupt business or break local laws. Find a little, metal, hinged container, of the sort that contained throat lozenges, mints, or pastilles. Place in the tin a pair of metal tweezers (old ones that no longer grip very well are fine), a few wooden safety matches, and a photocopy of the chart below.

To burn-test, remove all of the matches and other materials from the tin, grasp the fabric snip firmly with the tweezers, hold the swatch over the opened tin, and set fire to the sample. Extinguish the match as soon as the fabric smolders or catches fire. Then note the color, shape, and speed of the resulting flame, any odors, and the color, consistency, and quantity of ash or other residue. Dispose of the thoroughly cooled burnt sample and match safely and properly. Check the following chart:

Wool	Curls away from the flame and burns slowly. May extinguish itself (a good fiber to wear during a plane crash). Smells like burned hair. Leaves a little, black, brittle bead.
Silk	Curls away from the flame and melts slightly. Burns slowly. Smells like burned hair. Leaves a soft, black ash.
Linen, Cotton	Ignites immediately on contact with flame (not good fibers to wear in a plane crash). Burns fast and leaves an afterglow when extinguished. Leaves a feathery, gray ash. Smells like burning paper.
Rayon	Burns without flame or melting. Leaves a light, fluffy residue. Smells like burning paper.
Nylon	Burns and melts into a hard, gray, round bead. Smells like celery.
Acetate or Triacetate	Flames and burns quickly. Melts into a brittle, black bead. Smells like hot vinegar.
Acrylic	Flames and burns rapidly with a hot, sputtering flame. Melts into a hard, black, irregularly shaped bead. Smells acrid.
Spandex	Burns and melts. Leaves a soft and sticky residue. Smells like chemicals.
Polyester	Pulls away from the flame. Melts into a hard, gray or brown round bead (a bead of plastic). Smells like chemicals.

Index

Index note: page references in italics indicate a photograph or illustration.